NORTHERN IRELA
AND ITS NEIGHBOURS
since 1920

36-54

Sandra Gillespie
Gerry Jones

Hodder & Stoughton

The rights of Sandra Gillespie and Gerry Jones to be identified as the authors of this work have been asserted by them.

British Library Cataloguing in Publication Data
A catalogue for this title is available from the British Library.

ISBN 0 340 62034 X

First published 1995
Impression number   10 9 8 7 6 5 4 3 2 1
Year   1999 1998 1997 1996 1995

Copyright © 1995 CCEA

Printed for Hodder & Stoughton Educational, a division of Hodder Headline Plc, 338 Euston Road, London NW1 3BH by Colorcraft Ltd, Hong Kong.

ACKNOWLEDGEMENTS

The publishers would like to thank the following for use of material contained in this publication:

Camera Press Ltd, 109 (left), 116 (top)
Mr Colman Doyle, Camera Press Ltd, 106, 115 (top left)
Century Newspapers Ltd, 94/95
Crawford Municipal Art Gallery, Cork, 8
Her Majesty's Stationery Office, 18, 19, 26, 28, 79, 91, 96/97, 99, 100, 103 (top), 114 (centre)
Mr Ian Knox, Fortnight Magazine, 138
Newtownabbey Methodist Mission, 52
Mr Harry O'Brien, Camera Press Ltd, 107
Pacemaker Press International Ltd, front cover, 58/59, 92/93, 103 (bottom), 104, 112/113, 117, 123, 127 (top), 128/129, 130/131, 132, 133, 136/137, 139 (left), 142 (bottom),145, back cover
Popperfoto Ltd, 73 (left), 75, 101, 115 (bottom)
Punch, 17
Mr Crispin Rodwell, 143/144
Mr Bill Rolston, 42, 43, 44/45
The Belfast Telegraph, 42, 43, 44/45, 46/47, 54 (top), 97/98, 108 (right), 120, 124, 125/126, 134/135, 139 (right)
The Daily Mail, 74
The Hulton Deutsch Collection, 3, 5, 20, 21, 25, 72
The Linenhall Library, 33, 83, 90, 127 (bottom)
The Londonderry Sentinel, 108 (left)
The National Library of Ireland, 6, 48, 63, 65, 73 (right)
The National Museum of Labour History, 87
The Northern Ireland Housing Executive, 50, 51 (left)

The Observer, 121
The Press Association, 119, 121, 140
The Public Records Office for Northern Ireland 13 (bottom), 18 (top)
The Ulster Folk and Transport Museum, 32, 54 (bottom), 80/81
The Ulster Museum, 14, 34/35, 37, 38, 49, 53 (bottom), 78
The Ulster Unionist Council, 85, 86 (top right and bottom right)
The Writers and Readers Publishing Company, 64, 67
Topham Picture Source, 61
Turner Entertainment Co, 53 (top)
Mr Martin Turner, 130 (left)

In addition the publishers would like to thank Peter Keogh of Hodder & Stoughton Educational, The Northern Ireland Council for the Curriculum, Examinations and Assessment (CCEA) for editorial work, The Northern Ireland Centre for Learning Resources (NICLR) for design work and John Cooney for illustrations.

The publishers have made every effort to trace the owners of material used in this publication. In cases where they have been unsuccessful, they invite copyright holders to contact them direct.

Contents

Part 4:
The causes and consequences of political unrest within Northern Ireland

Highlighted words, such as **Act of Union**, are explained in the Glossary, starting on page 146.

Foreword

This book is an attempt to help young people, and others who may read it, to come to terms with the historical forces which have operated within Northern Ireland and between Northern Ireland and its neighbours since 1920.

FORMAT AND METHODOLOGY

The chapters are divided into short sections, each dealing with an important event. Each begins with a brief background statement on the issue and suggests one or two questions as the main focus of study for the section. The major events of the period are described in chronological order, using short explanatory text amplified by extracts from historical documents, photographs, cartoons and sketches and a wide range of contemporary sources, quotations, opinions and historical analysis. On one or two occasions, the language of sources has been adapted to make them more accessible to pupils. In the vast majority of cases, however, the language used is original. Short captions have been added to each source by the authors to assist understanding, but it is recognised that some sources will require teacher mediation. Each section ends with a set of questions and activities designed to assist students in absorbing and analysing the information given from a range of points of view.

LANGUAGE AND TERMINOLOGY*

The terms Protestant and Catholic and unionist and nationalist have been used frequently in the text to describe the main groupings in Northern Ireland but readers should be aware that these terms are open to a range of interpretations.

• Protestant and Catholic, unionist and nationalist

The labels Protestant and Catholic are particularly misleading because they imply that the dispute is primarily religious, which it is not. Over the years also they have become even more misleading as peoples' allegiances and views changed. For example, when Ireland was partitioned in 1920, most, though by no means all, Protestants might safely be described as being in favour of maintaining the union with Britain while most Catholics preferred a nationalist solution, involving either Home Rule or total independence, possibly even a Republic. Today, although almost all Protestants continue to be unionists, and almost all Catholics tend to be labelled nationalist in outlook, many different shades of unionism and nationalism have emerged so that the umbrella labels are not so easy to apply. For example, there are a substantial proportion of Catholics who support the continuation of the union with Britain but who tend to be labelled by others as part of the nationalist community because they would not, necessarily, regard themselves as feeling part of the Protestant unionist community. Therefore, not all Catholics are nationalists in the sense of desiring a united Ireland, and not all unionists are Protestant.

• Loyalist and republican

The terms loyalists or republicans are a bit more clear cut, in that they tend to be associated with only a minority in either community who support the use of violence in pursuit of their objectives, although these terms are sometimes used much more broadly.

• The 'third community'

There are many people in Northern Ireland who do not want to be labelled. There are many people who refuse to state their religion on census forms, who do not vote along sectarian lines or who do not vote at all, and who are frustrated with or who reject many of the attitudes which are associated with either side of the broad divide. Some are partners in mixed marriages and people who have come from elsewhere to live in Northern Ireland. Among them are very many of the younger generation who have seen Northern Ireland locked in the politics of conflict all their lives.

The format and methodology of the book aims to assist young people to develop a critical and objective outlook and an appreciation of **all points of view**.

---

*The following discussion is based in part on K Boyle and T Haddon, *Northern Ireland: The Choice*, 1994, with the permission of Penguin books.

Part 1
THE CAUSES AND CONSEQUENCES OF THE PARTITION OF IRELAND

TIMELINE

DATE

1914   *Home Rule is passed by the British Parliament. (Its implementation is delayed by the outbreak of World War I.)*

1916   *The Easter Rising takes place in Dublin and many of its leaders are executed by the British.*

1918   *A general election is called in Britain and Ireland. It turns into a sweeping victory for Sinn Féin and independence.*

1919   *Dáil Éireann, an Irish Assembly, is set up by Sinn Féin to replace British rule. The Anglo-Irish War/War of Independence is fought as IRA violence is stepped up against the British.*

1920   *The Black and Tans and Auxiliaries arrive to assist the Royal Irish Constabulary to maintain law and order. Troubles begin in the North where the Ulster Special Constabulary/ B Specials is formed. The Government of Ireland Act becomes law.*

1921   *Northern Ireland Parliament opens in Belfast. The Anglo-Irish Treaty which creates the Free State, and ends the Anglo-Irish War, is signed.*

1922   *Civil war in the Free State breaks out over the Anglo-Irish Treaty. The IRA begins a campaign in the North.*

1923   *Irish Civil War ends with a truce.*

1924–25   *Boundary Commission meets to look at the Border but leaves it unaltered.*

Background:
Home Rule – Unfinished Business

1.1

SOURCE **A**

The strength of Ulster's economy in the early 20th century

The linen industry gave rise to an engineering industry making textile machinery, and by 1910 two Belfast firms .... monopolised the making of linen machinery in the United Kingdom, as well as having a good export trade. Serious shipbuilding began in Belfast in 1858 and by 1911 Harland and Wolff's shipyard was the largest in the United Kingdom and had just opened the biggest dry dock in the world .... Belfast and Ulster's economic dominance was clearest of all in industrial output and exports. In 1907 industries centred in the Belfast region provided £19.1 million of the total of £20.9 million's worth of manufactured goods, (excluding food and drink), exported from Ireland.

M Farrell, *The Orange State*, 1983, with the permission of Pluto Press, (adapted from L M Cullen, *An Economic History of Ireland Since 1660*, 1972)

Focus

Why and how did Ulster unionists oppose Home Rule for Ireland?

What effect did the Great War have on Home Rule?

After a rebellion in 1798 led by a group called the **United Irishmen**, an **Act of Union** was passed in 1800 which united the parliament of Ireland with the parliament of the United Kingdom with the result that, for the rest of the 19th century, Ireland was ruled from Westminster. In the 1860s, a group of Irish politicians began to seek Home Rule for Ireland. They wanted a parliament in Dublin to look after internal affairs, but leaving matters such as foreign policy to the parliament at Westminster. This **Home Rule movement**, led first by Sir Isaac Butt and later, by Charles Stewart Parnell, grew in strength and gained the support of most of the Liberal Party and its Prime Minister, Gladstone. But not everyone in Ireland was in favour of Home Rule, especially in the prosperous north-eastern counties of Ulster. Those opposed to Home Rule formed themselves into the **Unionist Party** with the support of the Protestant **Orange Order** and the **British Conservative Party**.

Ulster's prosperity

Ulster prospered after the Act of Union in 1800. Steam power was introduced into the linen industry in the mid-19th century. Belfast and its surrounding area had gained almost total control of the linen trade in the United Kingdom by 1900 and had built up a strong export market to many other parts of the world. Engineering and shipbuilding industries had also developed. The six counties of Antrim, Armagh, Down, Fermanagh, Londonderry and Tyrone contained almost half (48 per cent) of all the industrial workers in Ireland. As time went on the economic gap between industrialised Ulster and the rest of Ireland, which was mainly agricultural, became greater.

SOURCE **B**

The contrast between Ulster's economy and the rest of Ireland

*Belfast and its **hinterland** more than ever represented an outpost of industrial Britain in Ireland. Belfast was effectively one corner of a great industrial triangle which linked it with Clydeside and Merseyside – it was cheaper to transport goods by sea to Glasgow or Liverpool than to send them to Dublin by rail. Belfast was sharing to the full in the economic expansion of Britain and its massive trade with the Empire .... The contrast was striking with the rest of Ireland, which was overwhelmingly agricultural, its industries being service industries or agriculture-based.*

M Farrell, *The Orange State*, 1983, with the permission of Pluto Press (adapted)

SOURCE C

Attitude of Ulster employers to the link with Britain and the Empire

In the midst of this remarkable prosperity Ulster employers were more determined than ever to resist any move which might weaken or sever their links with Britain and the Empire – the more so as the home market could never hope to absorb their greatly increased production – and they were supported by the bulk of the overwhelmingly Protestant workers in the shipyards and the engineering industry.

M Farrell, *The Orange State*, 1983, with the permission of Pluto Press

Home Rule

Many people in Ulster feared that Home Rule might weaken important market and trading links with Britain and the British Empire and that a parliament in Dublin would be more concerned with the welfare of farmers than of Ulster's industrialists. The first Home Rule Bill in 1886 was defeated by a combination of Unionist and Conservative Party opposition and because some Liberals voted against their own party. The second Home Rule Bill in 1893 was passed in the Commons but was defeated in the House of Lords, where Conservative peers were in the majority. The general election of 1910 left the Liberal Party depending on the support of the Home Rulers to form a government. The Liberals, with the support of the King, forced through a Parliament Act in 1911 which ruled that the House of Lords could only delay by two years Bills passed in the House of Commons. The third Home Rule Bill passed the Commons in 1912, but the opposition of the Lords meant it would not become law until 1914.

The UVF and IVF

Unionists in Ulster prepared to use force to resist the introduction of Home Rule. Edward Carson, leader of unionist opposition to Home Rule, threatened *Ulster will fight and Ulster will be right*. Unionists began organising and drilling a private army, the **Ulster Volunteer Force (UVF)**.

Edward Carson signing the Covenant.

Twenty-five thousand rifles were landed at Larne in 1914. A similar group, the Irish Volunteer Force (IVF), organised to defend Home Rule. When the First World War broke out in 1914 Carson urged the UVF to join the British Army. John Redmond, leader of the Irish Parliamentary Party which favoured Home Rule, also urged the IVF to join Britain in the war effort. Many UVF and IVF soldiers died fighting for Britain but a small number of Irish Volunteers denounced the war.

The 1916 Rising

On Easter Monday 1916, a small radical group led by James Connolly and Padraig Pearse, seized the centre of Dublin and proclaimed an Irish Republic. After a week of fierce fighting, what became known as the **Easter Rising** was crushed and many of the leaders were shot. The execution of the leaders changed the attitude of many Irish people towards the rebels and their cause. Asquith, the British Prime Minister, and his minister Lloyd George were anxious to persuade nationalists and unionists to agree on an immediate Home Rule settlement. In order to achieve Home Rule Redmond was willing to accept the temporary exclusion of six Ulster counties but Ulster unionists demanded permanent exclusion.

ACTIVITIES

1 Use Sources A, B and C (pages 2-3) to explain why many in the north-east of the province of Ulster were opposed to Home Rule.

2 What events before and during the First World War may have influenced the British government's stance on Home Rule?

Artist's impression of the Rising.

The Decline of Home Rule:
The Rise of Sinn Féin

1.2

Focus

Why did attitudes towards Home Rule change so much between 1914 and 1918 and what effect did this have on the prospects for Home Rule?

By the time the Great War had ended in 1918, attitudes towards Home Rule in Ireland had changed dramatically. Home Rule had been acceptable to the majority of **nationalists** *in 1914 but, after the 1916 Easter Rising, popular support for an Irish Republic increased. Most people in Ireland now wanted complete independence but most Protestants in the north-eastern counties of Ulster wished to maintain the union with Britain.*

The rise of Sinn Féin

Although not many people had supported the armed attempt in 1916 to establish an Irish Republic, the execution of the leaders of the Rising shocked many people in Ireland. This led to increased support for a newly organised political party called '**Sinn Féin**' which aimed to establish complete independence for Ireland. Eamon de Valera, one of the leaders of the 1916 Rising, was elected Member of Parliament for West Clare in 1917 but refused to take his seat in the parliament at Westminster. Later that year he became President both of Sinn Féin and the Irish Volunteers. By the end of 1918, Sinn Féin had become a well-organised political party.

Eamon de Valera, President of Sinn Féin.

The 1918 general election

After the Great War ended in November 1918 a peace conference was convened at Versailles in Paris. The Conference recognised the principle of '**self-determination**', the right of small countries to rule themselves.

SOURCE *A*

Complete and absolute independence

This organisation of Sinn Féin aims at securing international recognition of Ireland as an independent Irish Republic .... We are all united .... We want complete and absolute independence .... there is no (thought) of having a monarchy.

Eamon de Valera on his election as President of Sinn Féin

A month after the war ended in 1918, a general election was held. In Britain, a coalition government of Liberals and Conservatives was re-elected. The Liberal leader, Lloyd George, became Prime Minister but his government was mainly Conservative.

In Ireland, the **1918 Parliamentary Reform Act** had more than doubled the Irish electorate. Farm labourers, urban workers and some women over the age of 30 voted for the first time. The result of the 1918 election was an important turning point in Irish history.

Table 1: Seats held by Irish parties at Westminster

	Sinn Féin	Home Rule (Irish Parliamentary Party)	Unionist
Before 1918 election	7	78	18
After 1918 election	73	6	26

- The overwhelming success of Sinn Féin in this election meant that, virtually overnight, it replaced the Home Rule Party as the main force in Irish politics.

- Support for unionists in the north-eastern counties remained strong.

ACTIVITIES

1 What do Sources A and B tell us about the aims of Sinn Féin in 1918?

2 Use the information in Table 1 to draw a graph illustrating the strength of the two main Irish political parties before and after the 1918 election.

3 What does your graph tell you about the change in nationalist attitudes to Home Rule and suggest reasons to explain this change in attitude?

SOURCE B

Sinn Féin election leaflet and posters

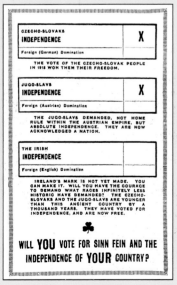

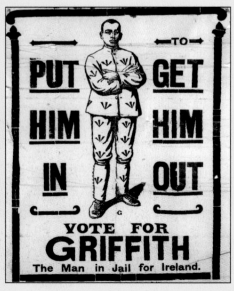

1918: Open Challenge to British Rule in Ireland

1.3

> ### Focus
>
> **In what ways did Sinn Féin's victory in the 1918 election affect British rule in Ireland?**

The results of the 1918 election in Ireland showed a dramatic change in attitude to Home Rule. Most nationalists now wanted Ireland to be completely independent from Britain. Sinn Féin candidates won a sweeping victory everywhere except Ulster and refused to take their seats at Westminster. Their statement to 'make use of any and every means available' to destroy English control of Ireland was a direct challenge to British rule in Ireland.

Dáil Éireann

On 21 January 1919 Sinn Féin invited Irish MPs of all parties to form a new Irish Assembly, the **Dáil Éireann**. Although Unionists and Home Rule MPs refused to attend, the Assembly met at the Mansion House in Dublin and declared Ireland to be an independent Irish Republic (based on the original **Proclamation of an Irish Republic** made at the beginning of the Easter Rising in 1916). Committees were set up to replace the British system of government.

Dáil Éireann's aims were to:

*   encourage people to ignore British rule;
*   sell **republican bonds** to raise money;
*   set up a Dáil court system;

SOURCE   A

Attempts at an alternative system of government

Perhaps the most successful of Dáil Éireann's activities .... was its system of Dáil courts or Sinn Féin courts.

J A Murphy, *Ireland in the 20th Century,* **1975, with the permission of Gill and Macmillan Ltd (adapted)**

SOURCE   B

A Dáil court hearing a case in Cork, 1920

- persuade local councils to recognise the Dáil as the legitimate government of Ireland;
- send a delegate to the **Versailles Peace Conference** to seek support for an independent Ireland.

In September 1919 the British government banned the Dáil. This forced the Dáil committees to go into hiding but they continued their work with some success.

The IRA

Many of the members and supporters of Dáil Éireann belonged to the Irish Volunteer Force which had taken part in the 1916 Rising. In 1919, the Volunteers became known as the **Irish Republican Army (IRA)**. The IRA was willing to use force to make the British leave Ireland. On the day the Dáil first met, two policemen of the Royal Irish Constabulary (RIC) were ambushed and killed by the IRA at Soloheadbeg. During 1919 the IRA organised into small groups called **flying columns**, launching hit and run attacks on individual RIC men and their barracks and avoiding capture by hiding in the community. By 1920 IRA attacks had spread to most of the country.

SOURCE

Painting of an IRA flying column

ACTIVITIES

1 What steps did Sinn Féin take in their attempt to take over the running of Ireland in 1919?

2 Use Sources A and B (page 7) to consider whether or not the Dáil was successful in its aims.

3 What does Source C suggest about the artist's view of the IRA and do you think it presents a realistic picture of the IRA? Give reasons for your answer.

4 Explain why the 1918 election is regarded as an important turning point in Irish history. Consider the changes that took place and the reasons for these changes. Your answer should include the following points:

  (a) changes in attitude to Home Rule after 1916;

  (b) the success of Sinn Féin in the 1918 election;

  (c) the formation of the Dáil;

  (d) the challenge to British rule in Ireland.

War in Ireland

> ### *Focus*
>
> **What was the nature of the war in Ireland and how was it viewed by both sides?**

*During 1920 and 1921, fighting continued in Ireland. This period is often called the **War of Independence** or the **Anglo-Irish War**.*

The Black and Tans

IRA violence increased, particularly against members of the Royal Irish Constabulary (RIC) many of whom resigned under the pressure of threats, **boycotts** and attacks upon their families. Unemployed soldiers were recruited in Britain and were sent to Ireland in March 1920 to reinforce the RIC. They became known as the **Black and Tans** because of the colour of their uniforms. Ex-Army officers, known as the **Auxiliaries**, joined them. The Black and Tans and Auxiliaries used ruthless methods against the IRA and often took revenge on local people and their property after an IRA attack. Their activities increased support for the IRA. By the middle of 1921, it was clear that neither side could win in this type of war.

Events in Ireland 1919-21

THE IRA	THE BRITISH
1919	
Jan. First ambush of RIC at Soloheadbeg.	
Sept. IRA attacks increase after the Dáil is banned. RIC withdraw to larger towns.	
1920	
RIC members resign in large numbers.	
IRA ambush Black and Tans who carry out reprisals against local populations.	***Mar.*** Black and Tans sent to reinforce the RIC.
Nov. Bloody Sunday - IRA kill 14 British agents.	***Aug.*** Auxiliaries sent to Ireland.
Black and Tans kill 12 people in retaliation.	30,000 troops and 11,000 police now in Ireland.
	Dec. Martial law declared in parts of Ireland.
	Government of Ireland Act partitions Ireland into two parts.
1921	
July	TRUCE DECLARED

SOURCE A

Republican attitude towards the use of violence

A state of war exists, and murder and violence against the English are not crimes until the alien invaders have left the country.

An t'Óglach (IRA newspaper) 31 January 1919

SOURCE B

British Government attitude to the war in Ireland

A small body of assassins, a real murder gang, dominate the country and terrorise it .... it is essential in the interests of Ireland (that) that gang should be broken up .... we have murder by the throat.

Lloyd George, British Prime Minister, 9 October 1920

ACTIVITIES

1   *What do Sources C and D reveal about:*
   (a) the Black and Tan views of the IRA and anyone who supported them?
   (b) the IRA views about the role of the RIC?

2   *What were the motives of the IRA and the Black and Tans in issuing these notices and what effect do you think these notices had on people at the time?*

SOURCE C

Black and Tan notice

DROGHEDA BEWARE

If in the vicinity a policeman is shot, five of the leading Sinn Feiners will be shot.

It is not coercion--it is an eye for an eye.
Are we to lie down while our comrades are being shot down in cold blood by the corner boys and ragamuffins of Ireland?

We say 'Never'. Stop the shooting of the police or we will lay low every house that smells of Sinn Fein.

(By Order)

Black and Tans

SOURCE D

Irish Republican Army Order

1. Whereas the spies and traitors known as the Royal Irish Constabulary are holding this country for the enemy-- we do hereby solemnly warn all prospective recruits that they join the R.I.C. at their own peril. All nations are agreed as to the fate of traitors.

By order of the G.O.C.

Irish Republican Army

SOURCE

Front cover of a popular history, R Bennett, *The Black and Tans,* 1959

A
FOUR
SQUARE
BOOK

2/6

their orders—
'Make Ireland
a hell for rebels
to live in'

THE BLACK
AND TANS
RICHARD BENNETT

3 Explain how the experiences of the Black and Tans and the IRA may have influenced their feelings and actions at the time.

4 Source E is the cover of a popular history about the Black and Tans published in 1959. Give reasons to explain whether you think that the book supports or opposes the role the Black and Tans played in Ireland in the 1920s.

5 In what ways do Sources A and B differ in their view of the fighting and suggest reasons to explain why the views differ so strongly?

6 The fighting in Ireland from 1919-21 was called by some 'The War of Independence' and by others 'The Anglo-Irish War'. What interpretation of the fighting is suggested by the use of these words and which groups are likely to have used these different descriptions of the war?

Troubles in the North 1920:
A Time of Uncertainty

1.5

Focus

What kind of fears did Catholics and Protestants living in Ulster in 1920 have and how did they react towards one another?

The War of Independence/Anglo-Irish War in the south increased northern Protestant fears. At the same time, Catholics in the north felt under threat as **sectarian** *violence increased.*

Troubles 1920

- Protestants feared that if the IRA and Sinn Féin war against the British was successful they would be forced into an Irish Republic.

- IRA activity was increasing in Ulster.

- In the local council elections in 1920 ten urban councils and thirteen rural councils were won by nationalists.

- Twelve Labour MPs were elected to Belfast Corporation, one of them topping the poll in the Protestant stronghold of Shankill. There was a concern among unionists that class-conscious workers might be more interested in wages and working conditions and might even throw in their lot with Sinn Féin.

- Attacks on Catholics increased.

There was serious violence in Londonderry between April and June 1920. In June, the UVF reorganised and took control of the city centre. Gun battles raged between the IRA and the UVF until 1,500 troops arrived at the end of June. A military **curfew** was introduced but violence continued. Forty people died in the violence.

There was serious violence all over Ireland in 1920 and some Belfast newspapers suggested in July 1920 that Protestants were being burned out of their homes in rural areas. These rumours inflamed sectarian attacks in Belfast, Lisburn, Dromore, Banbridge and other large towns. Hundreds of Catholics were forced to leave their homes and thousands were left without jobs.

Formation of the B Specials

To restore order, unionist leaders suggested re-forming the Ulster Volunteer Force which had originally formed in 1912 to oppose Home Rule. To avoid this, the government agreed to the setting up of an **Ulster Special Constabulary** in September 1920. This Special Constabulary became a mainly Protestant force and its part-time members, the **B Specials**, were distrusted and feared by the Catholic population.

SOURCE A

Call for Protestants to support Irish independence

Mighty changes are coming in Ireland. Do you Protestants wish to play a part in them? The unionist position can no longer be defended; your leaders are abandoning it .... do you not see that Englishmen are prepared to sacrifice you if they can secure the goodwill of the rest of Ireland? .... Ireland's right to decide her own future will come about whether the Protestants of Ireland like it or not.

Alderman Hugh O'Doherty, first Catholic Mayor of Londonderry, January 1920

SOURCE B

Unionist threats

We must proclaim today clearly that .... we in Ulster will tolerate no Sinn Féin – no Sinn Féin organisation, no Sinn Féin methods .... If .... you (the British government) are yourselves unable to protect us from .... Sinn Féin, and you won't take our help; we tell you that we will take the matter into our own hands .... I hate words without action.

Edward Carson at an Orange parade, Belfast, 12 July 1920 (Edward Carson led the unionist campaign against Home Rule and had supported the use of violence to defend Ulster against Home Rule.)

SOURCE C

Unionist appeal to Labour voters

.... these men who come forward posing as the friends of labour care no more about labour than does the man in the moon. Their real object .... is to mislead and bring about disunity amongst our own people; and in the end, before we know where we are, we may find ourselves in the same bondage and slavery as is the rest of Ireland in the south and west.

Edward Carson at an Orange parade, Belfast, 12 July 1920

SOURCE E

Demonstrations against Sinn Féin during 1918

SOURCE D

Nationalist view of the Ulster Special Constabulary

The Protestants are to be armed, for we (Catholics) would not touch your special constabulary with a forty foot pole .... Instead of paving stones and sticks they are to be given rifles.

Joe Devlin, Belfast Nationalist MP in the House of Commons, October 1920

SOURCE F

An early photograph of the Ulster Special Constabulary

B Specials, 1920.

1 Explain how the author of Source A (page 12) felt about the situation in Ireland in 1920.

2 The author of Source A, Alderman Hugh O'Doherty, was the first Catholic Mayor of Londonderry. Explain how a Protestant living in the city might feel about O'Doherty's speech.

3 What was the author of Source B (page 12) threatening to do and why might his threat have been taken seriously by the British government? Explain how a Sinn Féin voter living in Belfast might feel about Carson's speech.

4 Why do you think Carson spoke strongly in Source C (page 13) against the Labour movement?

5 Use Sources B, D, E and F (pages 12-13) to explain why Catholics feared the Ulster Special Constabulary.

6 Explain why Protestants and Catholics in the north reacted differently to the same historical situation in 1920.

Partition:
The Government of Ireland Act 1920

1.6

> ## Focus
>
> **What solution was suggested for governing Ireland in 1920?**
>
> **What were the reactions to this solution?**

Whilst the War of Independence continued in the south and sectarian violence continued in the north, the British government set up a committee to draw up a 'fourth' Home Rule Bill.

The search for a solution

The British government committee which was set up to find a solution to the situation in Ireland recommended that Ireland be partitioned into two parts, with separate parliaments in Belfast and Dublin. Agreement had to be reached on whether the Belfast Parliament should control six, or nine, counties in Ulster. It was finally decided that the six north-eastern counties Antrim, Armagh, Londonderry, Down, Tyrone and Fermanagh would be ruled from Belfast. On 23 December 1920 the 'Government of Ireland Act' became law.

SOURCE A

Map showing the percentage of Catholics in the nine counties of Ulster, 1920

SOURCE B

British attitude to 'the Irish problem', an historian's view

Behind the government's decision .... lay its constant anxiety to be free of Irish problems. The removal of responsibility for all local affairs to two home rule parliaments would ease the lives of British politicians.

M Laffan, *The Partition of Ireland 1911-25*, 1983, with the permission of the Dublin Historical Association

The Government of Ireland Act 1920: two Home Rule parliaments

An Act for the better government of Ireland:

- there shall be established for Southern Ireland a parliament;

- there shall be established for Northern Ireland a parliament;

- Northern Ireland shall be the counties of .... Antrim, Armagh, Down, Fermanagh, Londonderry and Tyrone;

- southern Ireland shall be .... the rest of Ireland;

- the powers of the parliaments shall be limited by Westminster;

- a **Council of Ireland** with representatives from north and south shall be set up;

- the Council of Ireland should work towards establishing a single parliament for the whole of Ireland.

Reaction to partition

In the north, a parliament in Belfast ruling six counties of Ulster was acceptable to most unionists. With a secure Protestant majority, they believed they could maintain and strengthen the union with Britain. Catholics who now found themselves a minority within the newly created state were violently opposed to partition.

In the south of Ireland, the 1920 Government of Ireland Act, offering a Home Rule parliament, was considered to be out of date with the wishes of the people and was almost totally ignored. In 1921, the British government was forced to agree separate terms with the south which replaced the Government of Ireland Act.

Although **partition** recognised the political realities of the time, the intention was that a Council of Ireland would *work towards establishing a single parliament for the whole of Ireland.* But the Council of Ireland never met and the parliament established in Belfast and later at Stormont governed Northern Ireland until 1972.

SOURCE

Ulster unionist reaction to partition

The Bill practically gives us everything that we fought for .... in 1913 and 1914. .... We see our safety, therefore, in having a parliament of our own, for we believe that once a parliament is set up and running well .... we should fear no one, and we feel that we would then be in a position of absolute security.

James Craig, Leader of the Unionist Party, House of Commons, 29 March 1920

SOURCE

Sinn Féin reaction

A minority in Dáil Éireann rejected this settlement. Its rejection hinged .... more on .... the question of an oath of allegience to the Crown than on partition .... To many .... it was partition that constituted the great betrayal.

C C O'Brien, States of Ireland, 1972

SOURCE C

Ulster nationalist reaction

They take the Catholic minority .... and place that minority at the mercy of the Protestant majority .... 340,000 Catholics .... are to be left permanently and enduringly at the mercy of a Protestant parliament in the north of Ireland.

C O'Clery, Phrases Make History Here, a Century of Irish Political Quotation 1886-1986, 1986, with the permission of O'Brien Press Ltd

ACTIVITIES

1 Using Source A (page 15):
   (a) identify the three counties of Ulster which were excluded from Northern Ireland and suggest reasons to explain why this decision was taken;
   (b) identify two other counties which might have justifiably been excluded from Northern Ireland because of balance of population and suggest reasons why this decision was not taken.

2 Using Sources B, C, D, E and F (pages 15-17) identify the attitudes and reactions of each of the following groups to the Government of Ireland Act: Britain, unionists, northern nationalists, southern nationalists.

3 Explain why Ireland was partitioned in 1920 and some of the intended and unintended results.

SOURCE

Cartoon on Partition

THE KINDEST CUT OF ALL.

WELSH WIZARD. "I NOW PROCEED TO CUT THIS MAP INTO TWO PARTS AND PLACE THEM IN THE HAT. AFTER A SUITABLE INTERVAL THEY WILL BE FOUND TO HAVE COME TOGETHER OF THEIR OWN ACCORD. (ASIDE) AT LEAST LET'S HOPE SO; I'VE NEVER DONE THIS TRICK BEFORE."

A Parliament for the North:
The Opening in 1921

Focus

How did different sections of the population react to the setting up of a parliament for Northern Ireland?

In May 1921, elections were held for the new Northern Ireland parliament. Unionists, under their new leader James Craig, won 40 of the 52 seats. In June, James Craig became the first Prime Minister of Northern Ireland. Against the advice of his ministers, King George V officially opened the new parliament at Belfast City Hall on 22 June. King George V and Queen Mary received an enthusiastic welcome on their arrival in the city. However, not everyone welcomed the King or the new parliament.

Commemorative poster.

SOURCE

Community violence

June 1921 had been a bad month in Belfast, especially in the York Street area, the violence here being characterised not only by heavy use of firearms but also by driving out families from mixed streets between the New Lodge Road and Tiger Bay. The UVF had been revived .... and (its) members .... had played a leading part in expelling Catholics from their jobs and homes in Belfast.

J Bardon, *Belfast: An Illustrated History,* **1984, with the permission of The Blackstaff Press Ltd**

A crowd of people in flight during rioting at the corner of York Street and Donegall Street.

SOURCE D

British reaction

I pray that my coming to Ireland today may prove to be the first step towards an end of strife amongst her people, whatever their race or creed .... I appeal to all Irishmen to pause, to stretch out the hand of forbearance and conciliation, to forgive and forget, and join in making for the land which they love a new era of peace, contentment, and good will.

The King's speech, 22 June 1921

King George V inspects the guard of honour at the opening of Parliament.

SOURCE B

Unionist reaction

The King and Queen had the most wonderful reception. The decorations everywhere are extremely well done .... with bunting and flags, and the pavement and lamp-posts painted red, white and blue .... as a sign of their loyalty .... precautions have been taken of every description, trusted men stationed in every house and on every rooftop. The scenes in the (Ulster) Hall were unforgettable, as the people could not contain themselves, and cheered for several minutes, and broke into singing the National Anthem.

Diary of Lady Craig, 22 June 1921

SOURCE C

Nationalist reaction

This so-called northern parliament is a danger to our liberties and a barrier to the permanent solution of the Irish problem, we (nationalists) can neither give it recognition nor lend it support.

Canon Crolly, Catholic priest, *The Irish News*, 5 April 1921

ACTIVITIES

1 What evidence in Source A and B justifies the King's advisers' concern about the his visit to Belfast?

2 What reasons does King George V give in Source D for coming to Ireland and how important do you think his presence and speech were?

3 According to Source C why were nationalists not in favour of a parliament in Belfast?

A Free State for the South:
The Anglo-Irish Treaty 1921

1.8

Focus

Why did both sides in the Anglo-Irish War agree to a truce and what were the results of the negotiations which followed?

*The Government of Ireland Act was generally ignored in the south and the war between the IRA and the British continued. In July 1921 a truce was agreed. Within a few months the **Anglo-Irish Treaty** was signed between the British government and the Dáil.*

Truce to treaty

The election of May 1921 was used by Sinn Féin to show the strength of its support in the south. All 124 Sinn Féin candidates were elected unopposed. But instead of attending the new 'official' Dublin parliament of southern Ireland created by the Government of Ireland Act, the Sinn Féin MPs again set up their own parliament, the second Dáil. The only MPs to attend the 'official' parliament were the four unionists elected for Trinity College, Dublin.

The Irish delegation.

Both the British government and the IRA realised that the military situation had also reached a stalemate and eventually, on 11 July 1921, a truce was agreed. Eamon de Valera and David Lloyd George met in London to discuss ways of finding a solution. They agreed to hold peace talks in London during October 1921 but de Valera decided not to attend the talks himself. Instead, Michael Collins and Arthur Griffith led the Irish delegation. The Irish had no experience of negotiations at this level and faced a skilled and experienced British team led by Lloyd George. After two months of disagreement and compromise Lloyd George presented a final set of proposals and told the Irish delegation that if they did not accept them he would begin an *immediate and terrible war*. The Irish delegates reluctantly signed the treaty without fully consulting their colleagues back in Dublin.

SOURCE A

Articles of the treaty

- *Ireland shall be known as the Irish Free State.*
- *The Irish Free State shall have its own government, parliament and army.*
- *The Members of the Irish Free State parliament shall swear an **oath of allegiance** to the King.*
- *Ireland shall remain in the British Empire and shall have the same status as the **Dominion** of Canada.*
- *A Governor-General shall be appointed to represent the Crown in Ireland.*
- *The British Army shall keep control of the ports at Cobh, Berehaven and Lough Swilly.*
- *The parliament of Northern Ireland shall have the right to opt out of the Free State.*
- *A Boundary Commission shall be set up to review the border between the Irish Free State and Northern Ireland.*

Articles of Agreement for a Treaty between Great Britain and Ireland, 6 December 1921

SOURCE B

'I signed my own death warrant'

Think – what have I got for Ireland? Something she has wanted for the past seven hundred years. Will anyone be satisfied at the bargain? Will anyone? I tell you this – early this morning I signed my own death warrant.

Extract from a letter written by Michael Collins just after he had signed the Anglo-Irish Treaty 1921

Michael Collins.

ACTIVITIES

1 *Examine Source A and identify those parts of the treaty likely to be acceptable and unacceptable to Sinn Féin which wanted complete independence from Britain.*

2 *Suggest reasons to explain why Collins signed the treaty and the reasons for his feelings as expressed in Source B.*

Reactions to the Anglo-Irish Treaty 1921

1.9

SOURCE

Pro-treaty reaction

We have come back from London with that treaty – Saorstát na hÉireann recognised – the Free State of Ireland. We have brought back the flag .... the evacuation of Ireland after 700 years .... the formation of an Irish Army .... We have brought back to Ireland equality with England .... If the Irish people say 'We have got everything else but the name Republic and we will fight for it' I would say to them that they are fools.

Arthur Griffith, signatory of the treaty, Dáil debate on the treaty, 19 December 1921

SOURCE

Pro-treaty reaction

To me this treaty gives me what I and my comrades fought for; it gives us for the first time in 700 years, the evacuation of Britain's armed forces out of Ireland.

Seán MacEoin, Dáil debates on the treaty, December 1921

SOURCE

Anti-treaty reaction

The two great principles for which so many have died – no partition and no control of Ireland by any foreign power – has gone by the board in this treaty.

Seán T O'Kelly, Dáil debates on the treaty, December 1921

Focus

Why did Sinn Féin split over the signing of the Anglo-Irish Treaty in 1921?

What were the results of the split?

Nationalists in Ireland were deeply divided about whether the treaty should be accepted.

The split over the treaty

Most ordinary people in Ireland were relieved that an agreement had been reached and the war had come to an end. Some Sinn Féin members felt so strongly about the treaty that the party split into two factions, those like Griffith and Collins who supported it, and the followers of de Valera who were against it. A long and bitter debate on the treaty began in the Dáil on 14 December 1921 and ended on 7 January 1922. The treaty was accepted by a vote of 64 to 57. De Valera and those opposed to the treaty walked out. De Valera was replaced as President of the Dáil by Arthur Griffith and the new **Free State** government was formed. Arrangements began for British withdrawal from Ireland.

ACTIVITIES

1 What reasons are put forward in Sources A and B to encourage the Dáil to accept the treaty?

2 What reasons are put forward in Source C to encourage the Dáil to reject the treaty?

3 Use the sources and the diagram to draw up a list of arguments for a member of the Dáil making a speech **either** supporting **or** opposing the treaty.

   Express opinions on:

   (a) peace;

   (b) the ideal of achieving a republic;

   (c) continued links with Britain; and

   (d) partition of the island.

COLLINS:
ARGUMENTS FOR THE TREATY

DE VALERA:
ARGUMENTS AGAINST THE TREATY

We have got peace which is what the people want.

We are able to set up our own government and rule ourselves.

An oath of loyalty to the King has no meaning.

This is a step towards independence. We will take other steps and become fully independent.

We are not in a position to start another war with Britain.

You may have peace but where is the Republic we have fought for from 1916?

Your powers are limited while you stay in the Empire and have the King as head of state.

We swore an oath of loyalty to the Republic and we will not swear an oath to the King.

Britain will continue to interfere in Ireland's affairs unless you remove her power completely.

We will still have British troops in our country.

The Response to Partition in the South: Civil War

1.10

Focus

What effect did the Civil War have upon the situation in Ireland, north and south?

The signing of the treaty led to a split in Sinn Féin and the IRA. Supporters of the treaty, led by Collins and Griffith who had signed it, joined the new national army to defend the Free State. Opponents of the treaty, led by de Valera, armed themselves and prepared to fight against their former comrades.

Brother against brother

In April 1922, the anti-treaty IRA seized the Four Courts in Dublin. The situation became very tense. A general election in June showed that most people in the Free State supported the treaty. With this support, and under pressure from Britain, Michael Collins ordered the Free State Army to attack the Four Courts. The IRA was driven out of Dublin. Bitter feelings developed on both sides and a **civil war** began.

The shelling of the Four Courts in Dublin.

The consequences of the civil war

IN THE FREE STATE	IN NORTHERN IRELAND
Arthur Griffith died, possibly due to overwork.	Many northern IRA members went south to fight in the **Civil War**.
Michael Collins was killed in an ambush in Co Cork.	IRA attacks along the border decreased.
There was bitter fighting for almost a year.	The threat to Northern Ireland's security was greatly reduced.

ACTIVITIES

1 Examine Source A and consider whether or not the IRA posed a genuine threat to the new Free State government. Give reasons for your answer.

2 What were the effects of the Civil War in the south upon the situation in the north?

SOURCE

A

Armed civilians on the streets during the Civil War

The Response to Partition in the North: Political and Security Measures

1.11

Focus

What actions were taken by the new government of Northern Ireland to try to ensure that the state would survive?

Britain had intended that a Council of Ireland would be set up to seek agreement on ways of uniting the country again. The 1920 border which partitioned Ireland was therefore considered a temporary measure by some of the British officials who set up the state of Northern Ireland and by most of the Catholics, who made up one-third of the population. Two of the counties of Northern Ireland had Catholic majorities, (Fermanagh 56.2 per cent and Tyrone 55.4 per cent) and the second city of Londonderry had a Catholic majority of 56.2 per cent. Most Catholics hoped that the promised Boundary Commission would redraw the border and make Northern Ireland unworkable. Because of their resentment of, or opposition to, the new state, most Protestants felt that Catholics could not be trusted.

Sectarianism

The first years of the new state were extremely violent. A renewed IRA campaign in the North and reports of the expulsion of Protestants from their homes in the south increased Protestant fears and suspicions in the north. Sectarian attacks increased. Between July 1920 and July 1922, 257 Catholic and 157 Protestant civilians were killed in Belfast and an estimated 11,000 Catholics lost their jobs in the shipyards, in engineering factories and other businesses with largely Protestant workforces. The new government responded to the worsening situation with the Special Constabulary (B Specials).

SOURCE A

An historian's view of the government's security and political measures

'The repressive nature of Northern Ireland government was not a deliberate plan to depress the Catholic minority. It can be argued that it was a response to the campaign of violence waged against Northern Ireland by the Irish Republican Army in 1922, with the connivance of some leading Free State politicians .... This threat to the very existence of Northern Ireland caused its government to take measures which have enabled critics to condemn it as a gerrymandered police state .... Catholics found their early suspicions of the state confirmed and they continued to opt out.

This refusal to participate, together with occasional IRA attacks on the border, enabled and encouraged Ulster unionists to remain defensively minded and to maintain the repressive apparatus erected to meet the emergency of 1922.

P Buckland, *Irish Unionism: Two*, 1973, with the permission of Gill and Macmillan Ltd (adapted)

A military post in York Street, one of the 1922 trouble spots.

Security measures

- The part-time Ulster Special Constabulary was strengthened to reinforce the Royal Ulster Constabulary (RUC).

- The Special Powers Act (1922) and the Offences Against the State Act (1924) were passed. These acts gave the government of Northern Ireland the power to arrest and detain people without trial.

Rioting in Belfast in August 1920.

SOURCE

B

The effects of gerrymandering of local electoral boundaries

The arrangement of ward boundaries .... has produced a permanent unionist majority which bears little or no resemblance to the relative numerical strength of unionists in non-unionist areas .... there is very good reason to believe the allegation that these arrangements were deliberately made and maintained to favour Protestant or unionist supporters in making public appointments and in manipulating housing allocation for political and sectarian ends.

Report of the Cameron Commission, 1969 (adapted)

(Left) Ballagh Bridge, Co. Fermanagh, destroyed by terrorists in April 1922.

(Far left) Mullagh Bridge damaged by a bomb during the terrorist campaign of 1922.

Political measures

The 1920 local elections left 25 local councils under nationalist control, many of which voted loyalty to Dáil Éireann rather than to the Northern Ireland parliament in Belfast.

- The government passed an Emergency Powers Bill on 6 December 1920 which gave them the power to appoint Commissions in place of any local authority which refused to recognise the government.

- **Proportional representation**, the system of voting for candidates in an election in order of preference, was abolished in Northern Ireland in 1922. This meant that fewer nationalists would get elected in a **'first past the post'** system.

- Local election boundaries were redrawn between 1922 and 1924 to ensure unionist control of local councils. The Cameron Commission, set up in 1969, revealed that in many areas where Catholics were in the majority, electoral boundaries were drawn to deliberately group large numbers of Catholic voters together so that they could elect fewer representatives. By contrast, the boundaries ensured that unionist voters were spread out across a number of electoral wards, allowing them to elect a greater number of representatives and therefore control local Councils even when they were in a minority. This tactic was called 'gerrymandering'.

- Only ratepayers were allowed to vote in local elections. One vote was allocated for every £10 paid in rates, up to a maximum of seven votes. This meant that wealthy business owners, who tended to be Protestant, could vote up to seven times while the poor, who tended to be mostly Catholic, had no vote. Poor Protestants were also unable to vote.

ACTIVITIES

1 Why were the first years of Northern Ireland's existence extremely violent?

2 What measures were taken by the Unionist government to ensure unionist control of the state and what effect did these measures have?

3 What reasons are suggested in Source A (page 26) to justify some of the measures put in place by the Unionist government in the period 1920–24?

The Boundary Commission 1924-1925

SOURCE A

Free State government reaction to maintaining the existing border

I firmly believe we have found the only solution in a very difficult situation .... It will remove obstacles which have been a source of bitter conflict between the peoples of Northern Ireland and the Free State.

W T Cosgrave, 4 December 1925

W T Cosgrave, Ramsay MacDonald and James Craig at Chequers, 1924.

Focus

Why did the Border remain as it had been drawn in 1920 and how did people react to this decision?

Under the Government of Ireland Act 1920 Britain had intended that a Council of Ireland would be set up to seek agreement on ways of uniting the country again. The Anglo-Irish Treaty of 1921, however, seemed to make the existence of Northern Ireland more permanent in two ways:

* it contained a clause which allowed Northern Ireland to opt out of the new Free State; and

* it made provision for a Boundary Commission which had the power to investigate and redraw the border in accordance with the wishes of the inhabitants, insofar as they might agree with economic and geographic conditions.

No change

The Commission was to have three members, one from the Free State, one from Northern Ireland and the third member was to be a **neutral** chairman. After many delays, the Commission started work in 1924 but its findings were leaked to an English newspaper. Fearing that uncertainty about the border might lead to violence, representatives from the three areas agreed to take part in urgent discussions to settle the location of the border. In December 1925, it was decided to keep the Boundary Commission's Report secret and to allow the border to remain unaltered. Nationalists in Northern Ireland had expected some areas along the border to be transferred to the Free State and nationalists north and south were disappointed the border had not been re-drawn. Nationalists refused to take any part in the parliament, join the police force or the civil service.

SOURCE C

Unionist government reaction to maintaining the existing border

I rise with feelings of deep thankfulness and relief .... I believe a new era will be opened in Irish history and that there is a possibility that .... much may be accomplished to smooth over the small but irritating difficulties that are bound to arise from time to time between two neighbouring States.

James Craig, December 1925

SOURCE B

Changes suggested by the Boundary Commission, 1925

Lough Swilly

Lough Foyle

Londonderry
St. Johnstown
LONDONDERRY
ANTRIM
Lifford
Strabane
Belfast
Castlederg
TYRONE
Pettigo
DOWN
Garrison
ARMAGH
Middletown
FERMANAGH
Rosslea
Newry
Derrylin
Clones
Forkhill
Crossmaglen
Carlingford Lough

——— The Border as it is

- - - - Line proposed by the Boundary Commission 1925

⇨ Arrows indicate direction of transfer

ACTIVITIES

1 What changes were recommended by the Boundary Commission and why was it decided by both governments to suppress the report?

2 How were the following groups likely to react to the decision to leave the border as it was: unionists in the north; nationalists in the north; the pro-treaty government in the south; and the anti-treaty opposition in the south?

The Longer-term Consequences
of Partition: A Divided Society

1.13

Focus

What happened in Northern Ireland over the next 50 years to deepen divisions between Catholic and Protestant in Northern Ireland?

When Northern Ireland was created in 1920, the majority Protestant population wished to retain and strengthen the link with Britain. Over the following 50 years Catholics in Northern Ireland came to believe that they were disadvantaged within the state.

Allocation of votes

- The effects of the fixing of electoral boundaries (**gerrymandering**) meant that the results of local elections became foregone conclusions. As a result, the bulk of candidates in local elections were unopposed. Between 1923 and 1955, the percentage number of seats which were not fought was:

  - rural councils   96%
  - county councils   94%
  - urban and borough councils   60%

- In 1945 the Labour government introduced universal suffrage, (the right of all people over the age of 21 to vote). The Stormont government did not extend this right to voters in Northern Ireland.

SOURCE A

Electoral boundaries, percentage population and Council representation in Londonderry

NORTH WARD

6,476 voters
39% Catholic voters
61% Protestant voters
8 Councillors

N

LONDONDERRY

Creggan Estate

Bogside

Walled City

SOUTH WARD

11,185 voters
90% Catholic voters
10% Protestant voters
8 Councillors

WATERSIDE WARD

5,549 voters
33% Catholic voters
67% Protestant voters
4 Councillors

River Foyle

SOURCE B

The link between houses and votes

The housing situation too was very bad .... only householders could vote. To give a person a house, therefore, was to give him a vote .... It would have been political suicide for it (the Unionist Party) to have given Catholics houses and votes.

E McCann, War and an Irish Town, 1974 (adapted)

SOURCE C

Discrimination in housing allocation

*There are several ways in which Protestant councils have **discriminated** against Catholics. One has been to put Protestants in better houses than Catholics but charge the same rent .... Another way has simply been to house more Protestants than Catholics. Of 1,589 houses built by Fermanagh County Council between the end of the Second World War and 1969, 1,021 went to Protestant families.*

Report on discrimination in housing allocation in Northern Ireland, The Sunday Times, 1972

- The Northern Ireland 'Representation of the People Bill' 1946 continued to restrict the right to vote to '**ratepayers** only' and retained '**multiple voting**', the right of businesses with large rateable values to have up to six votes.

Allocation of housing

It was generally easier for Protestant families in Northern Ireland to obtain houses.

- Housing was allocated by local councils which were mostly unionist controlled.
- A person's religion was often taken into consideration when they applied for a house.
- Protestants were often given houses before Catholics.

Allocation of jobs

It was generally more difficult for Catholics in Northern Ireland to find jobs, especially government jobs.

- A person's religion was often taken into consideration when they applied for jobs.
- Catholics were more likely to be unemployed than Protestants.
- Few Catholics obtained government jobs because it was felt they were not loyal to the Northern Ireland State. Between 1927 and 1972 95% of senior posts in the Civil Service were held by Protestants.

SOURCE D

'Employ good Protestant lads and lassies'

Roman Catholics .... were out with all their force and might to destroy the power and constitution of Ulster. There was a definite plot to overpower the vote of unionists in the north .... would appeal to loyalists therefore to employ good Protestant lads and lassies (cheers).

Speech by Sir Basil Brooke (later Prime Minister of Northern Ireland from 1945–63), 12 July 1933

SOURCE E

'The question of disloyal Catholics'

The amount of talk and print produced by my statement on the question of disloyal Roman Catholics is phenomenal. I would assure you, however, I have lost not one night's sleep over it. What I said was justified. I recommended those people who are loyalists not to employ Roman Catholics, ninety nine per cent of whom are disloyal.

Sir Basil Brooke, Londonderry Sentinel, 1962

Members of the Protestant Orange Order marching on the Twelfth of July in commemoration of the victory of King William III over the Catholic King James II at the Battle of the Boyne, 1690.

SOURCE F

Experience of a Catholic civil servant

The only Catholic to have achieved the office of Secretary of a Department through promotion from the junior ranks .... noted that while his colleagues invariably treated him correctly, and could in no way be accused of overt racism, many nevertheless accepted the discrimination against him as simply a way of life.

J J Lee, *Ireland 1912–1985*, 1990 with the permission of Cambridge University Press (adapted from P Shea, *Voices and the Sound of Drums*, 1981)

SOURCE G

Discrimination on the grounds of religion

INTRODUCTION CARD.   Class of placing

MINISTRY OF LABOUR, NORTHERN IRELAND.

ALFRED STREET

Order No......... Date......... Classn No.........

Employment Exchange   Phone No.........

To.........

In reply to your request for.........

I am sending the bearer, M.........
Please complete the space below and return this card to me as soon as possible, through the post, in the enclosed prepaid envelope.

.........193   H. G. STEVENSON *Manager.*

EMPLOYER'S REPLY.

Have you engaged the worker?.........

Date worker is to start.........

If the worker is not engaged please state overleaf the reason

Please impress business stamp.   Signature.........
E.O. 12.   Date.........193.....
N. Ireland.   P.T.O.

IMPORTANT.

Refusal of suitable employment is a disqualification for the receipt of Unemployment Benefit

In the public interest, therefore, you are asked to state fully why you did not engage the applicant.

Religion

Ministry of Labour, Northern Ireland introductory card, 30 September 1936

SOURCE H

Craig's attempts to involve Catholics in the running of the state

Craig .... was no bigot. He genuinely wished to reconcile Catholic and Protestant in Northern Ireland. He was even prepared to contemplate the possibility of a united Ireland in his own lifetime. But he found himself confronted at every turn by his own extremists and by the Catholic opposition .... Craig made a number of genuine, if limited, attempts to persuade Catholics to co-operate in the new administration. He reserved one-third of the places in the police force for them, and invited them to participate on the Lynn Committee of inquiry into education. When they failed to respond, he seems to have decided that future initiatives for conciliation must come from them.

J J Lee, *Ireland 1912–1985*, 1990, with the permission of Cambridge University Press

ACTIVITIES

1   *Examine Sources A to G (pages 31-33) Use the sources to explain why Catholics felt they were victims of discrimination.*

2   *What evidence is offered in Source H to suggest that some attempt had been made by James Craig in the early years to involve Catholics in the running of Northern Ireland?*

TIMELINE

DATE

1921   *The Northern Ireland Parliament opens in Belfast.*

1922   *Sectarian riots erupt, many Catholics are forced out of their jobs in the shipyard and engineering works.*

1929   *The Wall Street Crash takes place in the United States.*

1930s   *The Great Depression occurs with resulting high unemployment for Northern Ireland.*

1932   *The Outdoor Relief Strike takes place in Belfast; unemployed Protestant and Catholic workers briefly come together for a common cause.*

1935   *Sectarian riots erupt and troops are called in to restore order.*

1939   *The Second World War is declared; Eire remains neutral.*

1941–42   *The Germans blitz Belfast and Londonderry.*

The Economy of Northern Ireland in the 1920s

2.1

> ## Focus
>
> **What was the economy of Northern Ireland based on in the 1920s?**
>
> **How did it compare with the economy of the Free State?**
>
> **How did Northern Ireland survive economically after partition?**

Northern Ireland's industries experienced a boom after the First World War because of greater demand for goods which had not been available during the war. Prices rose and linen mills, farms and shipyards increased their output. At the time of **partition** *in 1920, the economy of the newly created state of Northern Ireland was at its peak. The boom period soon ended and by 1921 the situation had changed. Northern Ireland industry entered a period of depression that lasted for 20 years. Northern Ireland remained one of the most economically depressed areas of the United Kingdom.*

The Free State economy

The economy of the south of Ireland still remained heavily dependent on agriculture and continued to be underdeveloped in many ways. One of the biggest problems was the continued decline in the population which fell from 3.1 million in 1911 to 2.97 million in 1926, mostly due to emigration. This decline continued and was even more serious in rural areas. There was some small-scale industrial development but these found it difficult to compete in the open market. On the positive side, in a period of great difficulty across the world, the **Free State** economy did well to survive. A great deal of reconstruction was undertaken after the **Civil War**, budgets were balanced and taxation was held firmly in check.

The Northern Ireland economy

The six counties which form Northern Ireland cover about one-sixth of the area of Ireland (5,237 square miles). In 1926 the total population was 1,256,561, approximately one-third of whom were Catholic. Sixty per cent of the population lived in the greater Belfast area. The main industries in Northern Ireland at the time were: agriculture, shipbuilding, engineering and the manufacture of linen. Most of the factories, mills and shipyards were located in the east, close to the shipping ports of Belfast and Larne.

The Northern Ireland economy was possibly better off and more secure after partition than it might have been in a united Ireland under Home Rule. Northern Ireland did not become a separate economic unit cut off from the rest of Ireland and Britain. In fact, trade continued across the border

> ## SOURCE
>
> ### Economic links with Britain
>
> *Northern Ireland was never an economic unit, never likely to be 'economically viable' or self sufficient, and its economic decisions have always operated within the broader framework of central government at Westminster.*
>
> **D Harkness, *Northern Ireland Since 1920*, 1983, with the permission of the Educational Company of Ireland**

with the Free State, often illegally through smuggling, and economically Northern Ireland was treated as virtually another region of Britain. This provided a number of advantages:

- agriculture received help from British funds;

- Northern Ireland's goods were not taxed going into Britain; and

- the British government provided money to the Unemployment Fund.

The depression

The post-war boom began to tail off and all three main industries, shipbuilding, linen and agriculture, were soon to experience problems.

THE SHIPYARDS

- So many ships had been built by 1920 that the need for new ships decreased.

- Shipyards in the United Kingdom were faced with competition from new shipbuilding countries, such as Japan, the United States, Scandinavia and Holland.

Workers at the shipyard.

THE LINEN INDUSTRY

- Linen faced competition from new textiles such as rayon.

- There was less demand for linen clothing and underwear because of changes in ladies fashions.

- Linen became more expensive than other textiles.

- The number of workers employed in the linen industry declined.

A Spinning Mill, Belfast.

AGRICULTURE

- The world prices of farm products fell during the 1920s because farmers were producing too much and the demand for their goods was not increasing.

- Small farms in Northern Ireland had to compete with larger farms in Britain.

The main type of farming was **livestock** and this suffered less from falling prices than growing crops. Northern Ireland's farmers remained much poorer than those in Britain and many gave up farming during this period.

The main effect of the **depression** in the 1920s was a rise in unemployment. The number of people out of work rose steadily and the government was unable to attract new industries, such as chemicals, motor vehicles and electrical engineering, to Northern Ireland.

ACTIVITIES

1 One of the major questions following partition was whether the new Northern Ireland economy could survive on its own.

(a) How did the economy of Northern Ireland compare with the Free State's economy?

(b) Suggest reasons to explain why, despite the depression, Northern Ireland was able to survive economically in the 1920s.

Harvesting.

World Economic Depression

2.2

Focus

How did the Great Depression affect the economy of Northern Ireland in the 1930s?

The 1930s was the period of the **Great Depression** throughout the world. The United States of America was the largest market for goods produced around the world and many countries depended on selling products to America. When the economy of the United States collapsed, millions of Americans were left without work. To protect their remaining industries, the US government began both to restrict the amount of goods bought from other countries and to place heavy taxes on incoming goods. American banks also withdrew a lot of their money from European countries which were relying on it to build up their economies after the war. The result was that world trade collapsed and millions of people became unemployed. The Depression was so bad in Germany that money became almost worthless.

SOURCE A

Numbers employed and average wages

Linen employment figures

Year	Number employed
1916	90,000
1924	86,762
1925	70,421
1935	57,000

Shipbuilding employment figures

Year	Number employed
1920	30,000
1932	2,000

Average weekly wage

1920	87 shillings (£4.35p)
1925	47 shillings (£2.35p)

SOURCE B

How the Depression affected world trade

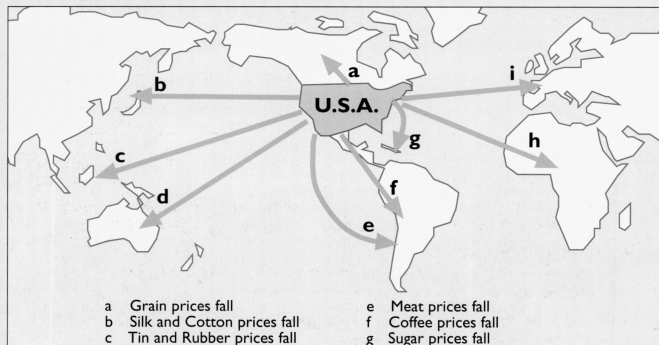

a Grain prices fall	e Meat prices fall
b Silk and Cotton prices fall	f Coffee prices fall
c Tin and Rubber prices fall	g Sugar prices fall
d Wool prices fall	h Cocoa prices fall
	i Europe's industry collapses

Rising unemployment

The collapse of the American economy and the Great Depression meant a collapse in demand for Northern Ireland's goods. In the worst years of the Great Depression, over one quarter of the Northern Ireland workforce was unemployed. In 1932, there were 72,000 registered unemployed. A further 30,000, mostly unemployed farm workers, were not included in the official figures because they were not registered in the government insurance scheme.

Without wages, the unemployed had to rely on claiming benefits to get money for their basic needs like food, heat, rent and clothing. The Northern Ireland government's policy was to keep social security payments in Northern Ireland in line with Britain. With rising unemployment, this policy was very expensive to maintain.

SOURCE C

Northern Ireland unemployment rates by industry, 1932

INDUSTRY	UNEMPLOYMENT
Building trades	39.2%
Distributive trades (shops)	17.6%
Flax and linen	23.5%
Food and drink	14.7%
Shipbuilding	57.0%
Tailoring/dressmaking	26.9%

SOURCE D

Percentage unemployment rates 1927–1945

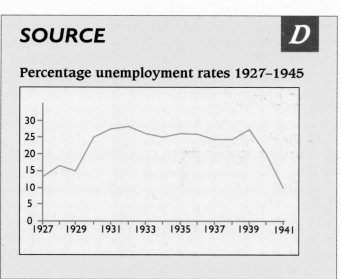

ACTIVITIES

1   Using the sources and the other information provided, explain how and why the shipbuilding and linen industries suffered serious unemployment during the Great Depression of the 1920s and 30s.

2   Suggest reasons to explain why:
   (a)   the ship building and the building trades suffered badly during the Great Depression;
   (b)   other industries listed in Source C suffered less unemployment.

3   Use Source D to identify:
   (a)   the year when unemployment rose sharply; and
   (b)   the length of time the Great Depression lasted.
   In which years was unemployment at its worst? Suggest reasons for these figures.

Social Unrest in the 1930s:
The Outdoor Relief Strike 1932

2.3

SOURCE   A

A view of the Poor Law Guardians

The Guardians were mainly drawn from the middle classes and reflected strongly the prejudices of that class .... They had strong religious beliefs and believed paupers, destitute as well as able-bodied unemployed, were being punished by God for some sin they had committed. They also believed that the destitute were scheming constantly to steal money from the ratepayers.

P Devlin, Yes, We Have No Bananas: Outdoor Relief in Belfast 1920-1939, 1981

Outdoor relief workers performing task work.

Focus

Why did Catholics and Protestants unite in 1932 in a strike to improve the outdoor relief system?

Poverty and hardship caused by unemployment was shared by both sections of the population and the Outdoor Relief Strike in 1932 illustrates the degree of hardship suffered by the unemployed. As unemployment increased, more and more people were forced to claim unemployment benefit from the government. This was paid for a short period of time only, usually just a few weeks. Thereafter the unemployed had to apply to their local Board of Poor Law Guardians for **outdoor relief**.

Outdoor relief

Although the government began to take some responsibility for the poor in the early 1900s, nevertheless, parts of the Poor Law, which had been set up 100 years before to provide for the poor and the homeless, were still in operation. Each parish had a Board of Guardians who ran the local poor-house or workhouse and administered the 'outdoor relief scheme' from money, or 'rates', collected from local businesses and house owners. The Board of Guardians tended to be middle class people whose aim was to keep the rates in their area as low as possible by making it very difficult to get work on a relief scheme, thereby keeping the numbers claiming relief as low as possible.

SOURCE B

The role of the Poor Law Guardians

The Guardians' duty was to discourage idleness and to create a spirit of independence since much of the money given to the poor was wasted .... these people (the unemployed) would make an effort to find work if they found they could not get relief.

From a speech by the chairman of the Belfast Guardians

- An unemployed person had to apply to, and then appear before, the Guardians and prove that he or she needed the relief work. Humiliating questions were often asked.

- The person was then '**means tested**' by relief officers who visited their homes to investigate their circumstances.

- People were sometimes told to sell their furniture or belongings before they could claim relief.

Outdoor relief work was very hard. It meant working outdoors for two and a half days on 'task work', such as road mending. The amount of money paid, called the relief rate, was low compared to proper wages. In addition, there were often not enough places on task work schemes and only those who did actual task work were paid in cash. Others were given tokens or 'chits' to exchange for food which meant that they had no money to pay rent and bills or to buy clothes, drink or cigarettes.

SOURCE C

Weekly relief rates in British cities

Northampton	*27s (£1.35)*
Bradford	*26s (£1.30)*
Glasgow	*25s (£1.25)*
Liverpool	*23s (£1.15)*
Manchester	*21s (£1.05)*
Belfast	*12s (£0.60)*

Outdoor relief workers striking.

The Outdoor Relief Strike 1932

On Monday, 3 October 1932, outdoor relief workers in Belfast went on strike to demand improvements in the relief system. The strike brought both sections of the community together in protest at the way unemployed people were being treated by the government and the Boards of Guardians. Over 60,000 people from all areas of Belfast marched to Custom House Square for a strike meeting. The protesters were addressed by strike leaders and politicians, including independent unionists, nationalists, the Northern Ireland Labour Party and the Revolutionary Workers' Group.

THE STRIKERS' DEMANDS:

- the ending of all task work;
- an increase in the rate of relief;
- payment in cash not in food tickets;
- payment of all street improvement work at trade union rates;
- outdoor relief to be given to single unemployed men and women.

SOURCE D

Reports of the protest meeting

Alderman Pierce said that he had come down the Shankill Road with the largest procession he had ever seen and as they passed Carrick Hill (a Catholic area) they were cheered .... That was the spirit of unity.

Tommy Geehan, the Strike Committee organiser said that they had been divided by .... politics and religion, but tonight they had Protestants and Catholics marching shoulder to shoulder.

The Irish News, 4 October 1932

The following day the strikers marched in protest to the workhouse where the Board of Guardians was meeting. The Guardians held talks with the strikers over the next week but the strikers planned a further protest march to the workhouse on 11 October. The government banned the march under the Special Powers Act and extra police were brought into Belfast to enforce the ban.

Rioting

More than half of the police force of Northern Ireland were on duty in Belfast on the 11 October 1932. Using batons, they broke up the march at each of the gathering points. **Rioting** broke out in many parts of the city as Catholic and Protestant strikers fought with police and damaged property. Paving stones were dug up and used by rioters to throw at the police. Reports of rioting on the Shankill Road suggested that shots were fired at the police and that the police opened fire on the Falls Road where the fighting was fiercest. Later that night, a curfew was imposed and quiet was restored. Two people had been shot dead and many more injured. Rioting continued the next day and barricades were erected in many areas.

The role of the government

The government gave the police the instructions to ban all marches and clear the streets. At the same time, it put pressure on the Board of Guardians to come to an agreement with the strikers. The Board of Guardians was summoned to a cabinet meeting and told to offer new rates of relief. On Saturday, 15 October, the strikers agreed to accept the offer and on Monday, 17 October, the strikers returned to work. The curfew was removed on the following day. New offices were opened to deal with people claiming outdoor relief.

Results of the strike

- The payments to married men increased by 150%.

- There was an end to food tickets as payment.

- Single men could be included in relief schemes.

- The Guardians changed the means test investigation.

Police in force in Berlin Street where several baton charges took place.

SOURCE *E*

Order Civil Authorities (Special Powers) Act Northern Ireland

Whereas there is reason to believe that assemblies of persons have been convened for the purpose of holding meetings on the 11 October, 1932, ... for the purpose of procession to the workhouse, Belfast. And whereas there is reason to believe that such assemblies .... will give rise to grave disorder and .... a breach of the peace.

Now, therefore, I SIR CHARLES GEORGE WICKHAM, DSO .... Do HEREBY PROHIBIT the holding of any such meetings or processions ....

ACTIVITIES

1 What were the causes and consequences of the 1932 Outdoor Relief Strike? STRIKE DEMANDS RESULTS OF THE STRIKE.

2 What is suggested in Source D about the relationships between Protestants and Catholics during the strike?

3 Describe the motives and actions of the following groups involved in the strike:
   (a) the Board of Guardians;
   (b) the strikers;
   (c) the government.

Interpretations of the Significance of the 1932 Strike

2.4

Focus

How lasting was the unity between Catholics and Protestants during and after the outdoor relief strike?

The 1932 Outdoor Relief Strike was seen by many people as proof that Catholic and Protestant workers could unite and end sectarianism. But, soon after the strike was over, Catholics and Protestants were once more divided by old fears and hatreds. By 1935, sectarian rioting and killing had returned to Belfast.

SOURCE A

Protestant and Catholic unity

The Outdoor Relief workers strike .... was the only moment when the unity of Protestant and Catholic workers in Belfast appeared to have actually come about.

P Bew and C Norton, The Unionist State and the Outdoor Riots of 1932, *Economic and Social Review,* **1979**

Support for the strike

The strike had been organised to force the government and the Boards of Guardians to provide more help for the unemployed. The protest was about money, food and working conditions, not about religious or political differences.

- Food was collected and given out to needy families.

- Aid was sent by Dublin supporters of the strike.

- Many Protestant churches set up **soup kitchens** to feed the strikers and their families.

- The Catholic Church helped poor Catholic families through the work of the Saint Vincent De Paul Society but did little else to support the strike.

Reaction to the strike

- The Catholic Church leaders condemned the strike as the work of **Communists**.

- The IRA may have been involved in shooting at the police during later rioting, but there is no evidence of their involvement in organising the strike or the marches.

- Speeches by unionist politicians warned of a republican plot and that Catholics could not be trusted.

- De Valera's accession as leader of the government in the south in 1932 was considered by many Protestants to pose a new threat to Northern Ireland's existence.

> SOURCE **B**
>
> **A striker's view**
>
> *The people were shoulder to shoulder for one thing and I think they realised it was only for one thing. Unity was very limited. The strike was not organised for a political purpose.*
>
> **R Munck and B Rolston,** *Belfast in the Thirties,* **1987**

> # SOURCE **C**
>
> **Comments on the role of unionist politicians and the Catholic Church**
>
> *The unionist politicians very quickly moved into Protestant **ghetto** areas .... saying to the ordinary working class people, 'Look you can't unite with these Catholics because .... they wanted to destroy the state of Northern Ireland and take us into a united Ireland'. Unfortunately, through fear, the Protestant working class believed these stories and very quickly the whole movement was divided again .... And I think the Catholic Church must bear some of the blame because they labelled it a communist front.*
>
> **The Troubles,** Thames Television, 1981

Women and children line up outside a Salvation Army 'soup kitchen'.

SOURCE D

The extent of unity between Catholic and Protestant, an historian's view

*The extent of co-operation between the poor of both religions during the outdoor relief riots of 1932 has been exaggerated and romanticised, and there is no evidence that **inter-communal** tensions were eased for more than a few days.*

J Bardon, *A History of Ulster*, 1992, with the permission of The Blackstaff Press Ltd

SOURCE E

The Prime Minister, Sir James Craig

If the mischief makers who had come into Belfast had any plans .... towards obtaining a Republic, they were doomed to disappointment.

B Barton, *The Blitz: Belfast in the War Years*, 1989, with the permission of The Blackstaff Press Ltd

SOURCE F

Coroner's inquiry

In a later inquiry into the riots, the city coroner commented that those involved were aroused, almost entirely, by the public speeches of men in high and responsible positions and that people were easily led and influenced.

The return of sectarianism

After 1932, Catholics and Protestants in Northern Ireland quickly drifted apart again. The worst sectarian riots since 1922 broke out in July 1935 and troops were called in to keep order. Rioting, shooting and burning lasted for over three weeks resulting in:

* 11 people being killed (mainly Protestant);
* 574 people injured;
* 367 cases of damage to property;
* 133 cases of burning of property;
* 300 families being driven out of their homes (mainly Catholic).

Wild scenes in Belfast streets. Irish Weekly Independent, July 20 1935.

ACTIVITIES

1 Using your knowledge of the strike from the previous section which of the interpretations of the strike offered in Sources A, B, C, D and E (pages 46-48) do you agree with. Give reasons for your answer.

2 To what extent do you think the view, expressed in Source F, that people were easily led and influenced is supported by other evidence?

3 From your understanding of the events of 1932 and before, give reasons to explain why Catholic and Protestant working class unity was short-lived and limited to this shared opposition to relief rates.

Housing and Health
in the 1930s and 1940s

2.5

SOURCE   A

Report to the Ministry of Home Affairs on North Queen Street, Dock Street, Henry Street and Whiterock Gardens

(The houses) were mere hovels, with people living in indescribable filth and squalor .... damp, mouldering walls, many of them bulging, rickety stairs, broken floors .... crumbling ceilings .... Housing conditions in Belfast are as bad as they can possibly be; gross overcrowding .... some remedial action is considered essential .... (it is) politically necessary to do something.

Dr Carnwath, Report to the Social Committee of the Belfast Corporation on the Municipal Health Service of the City, 24 December 1941

Focus

In what sort of conditions did people live and why was little done to improve health and housing conditions?

A survey in 1938 revealed that the death rate in Northern Ireland was 25% higher than elsewhere in the United Kingdom, due mainly to poverty. Poor housing, bad public health and poor medical services bred illness and disease and women and children, in particular, suffered from poor health standards.

Housing

Most of the housing in Belfast had been built in the 19th century when the city began to expand rapidly as an industrial centre. Crowded, narrow streets of small terraced houses were built close to linen mills and factories. Some of the older houses dated back to the 1770s. By the 1930s, many were in a very bad condition. Most were tiny, four roomed houses packed into **back-to-back streets** with an outside toilet but no bathrooms. Crowded into these conditions were large families paying high rents. The government took no action to improve housing until 1941 when the Blitz damaged many areas and exposed the very poor housing conditions. Government reports revealed the scale of the problem.

Lavinia Street, 1938.

Many small farmhouses and cottages in the countryside were also in bad condition in the 1930s. Reports on rural living conditions highlighted some of the problems:

Government action on housing

At the time, the government in Britain was giving grants of £200 million to remove slums and build new houses but, due partly to a lack of government money in Northern Ireland, only £3 million was paid towards new housing. Although 10,000 houses were condemned in 1936 as unfit to live in, no

A typical country cottage.

action was taken to demolish them. The Northern Ireland government had financial difficulties and was both depending on money from Westminster and relying on private housing schemes to build houses. In 1939, for example, 30,000 houses were built for private sale or rent. The Councils blamed the government for not helping to build houses for the poor.

A typical cottage equipped with only a cold water supply.

Health

Poor living conditions and inadequate diets resulted in illness and deformity in young children. In the late 1930s, roughly 800 babies died in Belfast each year. By 1940, the proportion reached one in eight; about twice the figure for Liverpool or Manchester. Many babies died at birth. Children whose parents were unemployed were found to be lighter and smaller than children whose parents had jobs. Mother and baby care was very poor by modern standards and the risk of death when giving birth was 60% higher than in Britain. Working class women, often existing on inadequate diets had to work long hours during pregnancy. They could not afford to pay doctor's bills and often sacrificed their own health to keep the family fed and healthy. Men's health also suffered as a result of poor housing and diet. The worst killer disease was **tuberculosis**, or TB, a lung disease which was thought to be the cause of 49% of all deaths between the ages of 15 and 25.

Government response

Much of the death and illness in Belfast might have been avoided if medical services and health education had been better. The government could not afford to provide more money for health services and it would not force

SOURCE D

Poor diet

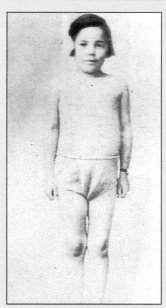

*Severe **malnutrition** was not uncommon in children. Fortunately, with proper care and a nutritious diet, this child recovered.*

E Allen, *Young in the Twenties*, 1988, with the permission of A & C Black

local councils to improve public health. The Belfast Corporation and the Board of Guardians believed it was not their job, but the job of parents, to take greater care of their families.

SOURCE

Children being given ultra violet treatment, Newtownabbey Methodist Mission

At the North Belfast Mission, undernourished children were given ultra-violet treatment for rickets, caused by vitamin D deficiency. The dark glasses protected their eyes from the glare.

SOURCE F

Women's health

The death rate of mothers giving birth actually rose by 1/5th between 1922 and 1939 .... In the late 1930s roughly 800 babies died in the city each year .... one out of every ten births.

B Barton, *The Blitz: Belfast in the War Years*, 1989, with the permission of The Blackstaff Press Ltd (adapted)

Dr Deeny in his study found that all women, employed or unemployed, were less tall than they ought to have been, heavier than was healthy, had weak blood, bad posture and poor skin colour.

R Munck and B Rolston, *Belfast in the Thirties*, 1987

ACTIVITIES

1 How do the visual sources illustrate the nature of the housing problem in Belfast?

2 In what ways were the housing problems in city and country similar and different?

3 From the sources and other information identify the causes of poor health in the Thirties under the following headings:
   (a) social conditions;
   (b) economic conditions;
   (c) lack of political action.

4 Explain why the authorities felt it was not their responsibility to improve health care in the Thirties.

Social Change

Focus

What changes occurred in the Thirties and how did they improve life?

Although many people were out of work for many years during the Thirties, some were unemployed only for short spells of time. Even at the height of the depression, only one quarter of the workforce was unemployed and social changes helped to improve the quality of life for everyone in Northern Ireland.

- By 1935, the cinema had become very popular and Belfast had 35 cinemas.

- Nearly half the families in Northern Ireland owned a radio by 1939.

- One family in seven possessed a car in 1937, compared to one family in sixty in 1917.

- Electricity use in 1938 had increased to three times that of 1932.

- Sporting activities, such as soccer, Gaelic games, motor sports and greyhound racing flourished throughout the Thirties.

Advertisement for Gone with the Wind. © 1967 Metro-Goldwyn-Mayer Inc. Used with the permission of Turner Entertainment Co. All rights reserved.

The Broadway cinema.

Football action from the 1930s shows Joe Bambrick displaying his skills.

SOURCE A

Social improvements in the Thirties

During the inter-war years, conditions for the vast majority of the population improved substantially .... Throughout Northern Ireland a measurable improvement took place in health, housing, life expectation and the overall quality of life. Electricity generation proceeded rapidly .... and consumption trebled over the next six years .... Leisure activities became more varied.

B Barton, *The Blitz: Belfast in the War Years*, 1989, with the permission of The Blackstaff Press Ltd

THE AUSTIN 7 SALOON DE LUXE £128

The Austin 7.

ACTIVITIES

1 According to Source A, in what ways did life improve during the Thirties?

2 What evidence in this section suggests that the Thirties was a period of progress for some people?

3 Suggest reasons why sport and leisure activities greatly increased in popularity during the Thirties.

4 Do you think it correct to say that the Depression or the improvements affected everyone in the same way? Give reasons for your answer.

The Effects of the War 1939-1945

SOURCE

Reaction of people in the countryside to the evacuees

They were totally unprepared for such numbers and the type of people arriving. The whole town is horrified by the filth of these evacuees and by their filthy habits and take-it-for-granted attitude .... The smell is awful .... They don't even use the lavatory, they just do it on the floor, grown-ups and children.

The Voice of Ulster, Ulster Unionist Party, January 1948.

SOURCE

Wealthy evacuees in a County Donegal hotel during the Blitz

Last year it was only half-full and those wearing evening dress were in a minority. This year it is crowded out, mainly with Belfast's wealthier citizens, and about 75 per cent are in evening wear. In fact the display of jewellery and furs is terrific.

Ulster 1960, HMSO

Focus

How did the war expose poor conditions and what was the government's response to poverty?

When war came in 1939 it had the effect of exposing the poverty, ill health and living standards of the poor in Northern Ireland.

The Blitz 1941

The Second World War began in September 1939. In April and May 1941, when German aircraft bombed Belfast and Londonderry, it became obvious that the government in Northern Ireland had not prepared for the war. There were not enough air raid shelters and anti-aircraft weapons with the result that the German air raids caused great suffering and damage. Some people chose to flee Belfast, night after night, to sleep in the surrounding

Child evacuees.

German bombers over Belfast, April 1941.

hills in case the German bombers returned. Thousands of others, rich and poor, fled to live in the country and small towns. Their war experiences brought people together, but as one historian described it, *The citizens of Belfast were united not by common love but by grief and common fear.* Looking after the evacuees put great strain on those who had to house them. The condition of the poorest families from Belfast shocked their new hosts in the countryside.

> ## SOURCE
>
> ### Criticism of the Minister for Public Safety
>
> *Will he go to the barns and sheughs to see the people of Belfast lying on damp ground? Will he come to Hannahstown and the Falls Road? The Catholics and Protestants are going up there mixed .... and they all say the same thing, that the government is no good.*
>
> **From a speech by Tommy Henderson, Independent Unionist MP, at Stormont, May 1941.**

What did the government do?

The Blitz showed up the poor housing, health and living conditions in Belfast and the government was blamed. During wartime, it had to take control of many aspects of everyday life, such as rationing food and fuel and many people hoped that these new powers might be used after the war to improve peoples' lives. The Prime Minister, J M Andrews, who had replaced Lord Craigavon in 1940, however, was very conservative and reluctant to prepare for change after the war. In 1943, Sir Basil Brooke, the new Prime Minister, set up committees to report on housing, health and living conditions. But it was the new Labour government in Britain after 1945 that introduced great changes and forced the Northern Ireland government to do the same.

> ## ACTIVITIES
>
> 1 In what way did the German bombing of Belfast help reveal the extent of poverty?
>
> 2 What do Sources A and B (page 55) reveal about the gap that existed between rich and poor in Northern Ireland?
>
> 3 Write a speech for Tommy Henderson MP which criticises the government's attitude towards the poor in 1941.
>
> 4 The Second World War is seen as a turning point in the social history of Northern Ireland. Explain why this is so.

TIMELINE

DATE	
1921	The Free State is formed after the Anglo-Irish Treaty is signed.
1924–25	The Boundary Commission meets to look at the Border.
1931	The Statute of Westminster becomes law.
1932	De Valera becomes Prime Minister of the Free State. The economic war between Britain and the Free State begins.
1937	New Eire Constitution is agreed.
1938	Britain returns the treaty ports to Irish control. The economic war ends with the 1938 Anglo-Irish Agreement.
1939	The Second World War is declared; Eire remains neutral.
1940	Britain offers to end partition in exchange for Eire's entering the War. (De Valera refuses.)
1945–50	The welfare state is set up by the post-war British government.
1949	De Valera declares the Republic of Ireland. The Government of Ireland Act is introduced.
1956	New IRA campaign in the North begins.
1962	IRA abandons its campaign due to lack of support in the North.

The Free State and Relationships 1920-1932

3.1

SOURCE

The Irish Free State Constitution 1922

- *The Free State is a member of the British Commonwealth of Nations.*

- *All powers of government and authority comes from the people of Ireland.*

- *The national language of the Irish Free State is the Irish language, but the English language will have equal status.*

- *The parliament (Oireachtas) will have two houses, the Dáil Éireann and the Seanad Éireann (Senate).*

- *The head of the government is called the President.*

- *The head of the Free State is the British King.*

- *All members of parliament will take an oath of allegiance to the King.*

- *The King's representative in Ireland is the Governor-General.*

SOURCE

Power of a Dominion's parliament

The parliament of a Dominion shall have power to remove or change any existing or future Act of Parliament of the United Kingdom.

Extract from the Statute of Westminster, 1931

Focus

What difficulties faced the new Free State government in its relations with Britain and Northern Ireland?

When the Dáil accepted the treaty in January 1922, **Sinn Féin** split into two factions: those who agreed with the treaty led by Collins and Griffith, and those who opposed it, led by de Valera. De Valera resigned as President of the Dáil and was replaced by Arthur Griffith who, along with Michael Collins and others who supported the treaty, set up a provisional government to rule the Free State. The first **Free State** government had problems, such as a Civil War with the anti-treaty group and establishing relations with its neighbours.

Creating the Free State

The new government quickly took over control from the British authorities and British troops and officials started to leave Ireland. Griffith died and Collins was murdered in August 1922 by anti-treaty forces. A truce in the Civil War was eventually declared, leaving W T Cosgrave and the newly formed **Cumann na nGaedheal** party to govern the Free State for the next ten years.

Agreement needed to be reached on a Constitution, (the rules and structures for governing the new state) so that a permanent government could be established.

Relationship with the North: the Boundary Commission

Under the **Government of Ireland Act 1920**, which set up Northern Ireland, the British had intended that a **Council of Ireland** would seek agreement on ways of uniting the country again. The treaty, however, seemed to make the existence of Northern Ireland more permanent by making provision for a Boundary Commission which, it was believed, would transfer the bulk of the north's Catholics to the south, and negotiate better conditions for the rest. But, when the time came, it was decided to keep the Boundary Commission's report secret and to allow the border to remain unaltered. Nationalists north and south were disappointed the border had not been re-drawn.

Relationship with Britain: the Statute of Westminster

Cosgrave's government was criticised constantly by de Valera's party, Fianna Fáil, for being influenced too strongly by Britain. While Cosgrave wanted to increase the Free State's independence he also sought to remain on friendly terms with Britain while working with other Commonwealth countries to gain more independence. Between 1922 and 1932 the Free State showed its independence by:

- becoming a member of the League of Nations;

- sending ambassadors to many countries;

- signing the **Commonwealth** Conference declaration of 1926 which forced Britain to recognise the equality of all members of the Commonwealth;

- playing a major part in getting Britain to accept the 1931 Statute of Westminster which reduced Britain's influence in the domestic affairs of the Commonwealth countries.

(Above) W T Cosgrave, President of the Executive Council of the Irish Free State 1922–32.

(Left) The British Army leaving the Free State 1922.

ACTIVITIES

1 What difficulties did the Free State face in 1922?

2 Look at Source A.
   (a) Which two clauses in the Constitution do you think would most displease a Sinn Féin supporter?
   (b) Why do you think it is unlikely that a member of Sinn Féin would support the Constitution?

3 How do you think the decision to leave the border unchanged affected:
   (a) relations between Northern Ireland and the Free State?
   (b) the popularity of de Valera's Fianna Fáil party in the Free State?

4 Using Source B, write a speech for Cosgrave explaining to the electorate why the Statute of Westminster is an important step in winning independence for the Irish Free State.

The Return of de Valera in 1932

Focus

Why was Britain worried about de Valera becoming the new leader of the Free State in 1932?

How did de Valera reduce Britain's influence in the 26 counties?

Anti-British feeling, and the desire for a Republic, remained strong in the Free State. Cosgrave was criticised for co-operation with Britain and blamed for the country's poor economic condition. In the 1932 election de Valera's Fianna Fáil party won most seats and de Valera became leader of the new government. Britain and Northern Ireland watched the developments in the Free State with concern.

De Valera's relations with Britain

Eamon de Valera had resigned from the Dáil in 1922 rather than accept the treaty and had refused to take the oath of allegiance to Britain in 1927. His opposition to British influence in Ireland continued throughout the 1920s.

De Valera and a group of Fianna Fáil TDs leaving the Dáil after refusing to take the oath of allegiance in 1927.

SOURCE A

'Squeezing England out'

Ignoring as far as possible any conditions in the treaty .... (ours is) a policy of squeezing England out .... Breaking the treaty by .... smashing (the oath) first and then forcing England to put up with .... changes or revise the treaty.

Eamon de Valera, 21 June 1923

SOURCE B

Election Manifesto for Fianna Fáil 1932

Aims of Fianna Fáil:

- *the revival of the Gaelic language;*
- *the end of partition;*
- *the abolition of the oath of allegiance to the British Crown;*
- *the suspension of **annuity payments** (yearly land payment to Britain);*
- *the introduction of **tariffs** (taxes) to protect Irish agriculture, industry and trade.*

ACTIVITY

1 Use Sources A and B to explain why the British government was concerned about de Valera becoming the leader of the Free State government.

The new Fianna Fáil government, 1932.

From Free State to Eire:
The 1937 Constitution

3.3

Focus

What changes did de Valera make to weaken the link with Britain and the Commonwealth?

What was the reaction inside and outside Eire to the 1937 Constitution?

Once in office, de Valera began steadily to remove the terms of the treaty that gave Britain influence in the Free State.

Dismantling the treaty 1932–37

- From 1932 land annuities were no longer sent to Britain.

- The oath to the King was abolished in 1933.

- The powers of the Governor-General were reduced in 1933 and the post was abolished in 1937.

- De Valera stopped the Irish using the Privy Council, (the highest appeals court in the British Isles), to appeal against decisions made in Irish courts.

- In 1936, the King's authority in the Free State was removed by the **External Relations Act**. However, the Free State continued to recognise the King as the Head of the Commonwealth as opposed to the Head of the Free State.

Cartoon of de Valera showing him dismantling the treaty.

SOURCE   A

Bunreacht na hÉireann

Article 2
The national territory consists of the whole of the island of Ireland, its islands and territorial seas.

Article 3
While maintaining the right to rule all thirty-two counties in Ireland, the laws passed by the Dublin parliament will apply only to the twenty-six counties until Ireland is reunified.

Article 8
The Irish language is the first official language. The English language is recognised as the second official language.

Article 41
The State forbids divorce or the remarriage of persons divorced elsewhere ....

Article 44
The State recognises the special position of the Holy Catholic Apostolic and Roman Church as the guardian of the Faith professed by the great majority of the citizens .... and the Church of Ireland, the Presbyterian Church, the Methodist Church, the Society of Friends, the Jewish congregations and the other denominations existing in Ireland.

Article 45
.... guarantees freedom of conscience to every citizen and prohibits religious discrimination ....

The Irish Constitution 1937

The British government was too concerned about the crisis created by the abdication of King Edward VIII, over his affair with Mrs Simpson, an American divorcee, to worry about de Valera's External Relations Act. It protested, but the Irish ignored the protests and the British took no further action.

The 1937 constitution

In 1937, a new constitution (**Bunreacht na hÉireann**) was produced which made the 26 counties a republic in everything but name. The Constitution suggested:

- changing the Free State's name to Eire;
- using the Irish name **Taoiseach** (Prime Minister), instead of President, for the leader of the government;
- electing a new Head of State who would be given the title of President.

A referendum was held in the Free State and the new Constitution was narrowly accepted. The new Irish Constitution created great interest in Commonwealth countries. De Valera decided Ireland would continue to be a member of the Commonwealth in the hope that this link with Britain might make it easier to bring an end to partition.

Douglas Hyde, the first President of Eire under the 1937 Constitution.

SOURCE **B**

Britain's view of the 1937 constitution

His Majesty's government .... (is) prepared to treat the new Constitution as not effecting a great change in the position of the Irish Free State.

The Irish Press, 31 December 1937

SOURCE **C**

Commonwealth view of the 1937 constitution

The Free State Constitutional proposals are of no great importance and they should not be taken as effecting a fundamental change in the position of the Free State as a Member of the Commonwealth.

W L MacKenzie King, The Irish Press, 19 April 1937

SOURCE **D**

Northern Ireland's view of the 1937 constitution

The effect of bringing into force this new Constitution in the Irish Free State will be to strengthen .... the determination of Ulster to resist all attacks from there (Eire) and make the links between Britain and ourselves stronger.

The Irish Press, 31 December 1937

SOURCE E

An historian's view of the 1937 constitution

Mr de Valera .... deliberately did not write into the constitution the one word (republic) which, of all others, was anathema to the men of the north. 'If the Northern problem were not there' Mr de Valera admitted in debate 'in all probability there would be a flat, downright proclamation of a republic in this Constitution'.

The broad toleration revealed in clauses (44 and 45) were, at least in part, ... to reassure the minority within the 26 counties and also to convince doubting Protestants in the six counties (if, indeed, any convincing was possible) that **Home Rule** *had not, after all, meant Rome Rule.*

F S L Lyons, *Ireland Since the Famine*, 1971, with the permission of Weidenfeld and Nicolson Publishers (adapted)

SOURCE F

An historian's view of the 1937 constitution

De Valera's declared concern for Ulster sentiment on the issue of the Republic seems curious in view of the fact that the Constitution contained numerous clauses bound to be repugnant to any self-respecting Protestant.

The resentment (among Protestants in the north over Article 44) was more retrospective than contemporary .... Non-Catholics could find more substantive cause for concern in other features (such as Article 41 which forbade divorce). The divorce provisions would not in practice have affected many people, north or south, at that time. But non-Catholics could feel that in principle they restricted liberty of conscience. When considered with the ban on the importation and sale of contraceptives, it was difficult to avoid the impression that the state considered it a duty to impose specifically Catholic doctrine on all its citizens, irrespective of their personal convictions.

J J Lee, *Ireland 1912–1985*, 1990, with the permission of Cambridge University Press

ACTIVITIES

1   Explain the way in which the relationship between Britain and the Free State changed between 1932 and 1936.

2   What changes did the Constitution of 1937 introduce?

3   Use Sources A to D (pages 64-65) to explain how the following groups reacted to the new Free State Constitution:

(a)   the British government;

(b)   the members of the Commonwealth;

(c)   Northern Ireland.

4   In what ways do the two historians quoted in Sources E and F differ in their views of the reaction of northern Protestants to the 1937 constitution? Give reasons for your answer, noting also the dates on which the books were published.

5   J J Lee suggests in Source F that the resentment (among Protestants in the north over Article 44) came about afterwards rather than at the time. Explain what you think he meant by this.

The Economic War 1932-1938

> ## Focus
>
> **What were the causes of the economic war?**
>
> **How did the economic war affect Britain, Northern Ireland and the Free State?**

*Britain and the Free State had been close trading partners but in 1932, both countries put import duties on the others' goods. The trade dispute which followed lasted from 1932 to 1938 and became known as the **economic war**, during which relations between de Valera's Free State government and its neighbours deteriorated.*

Land annuities

At the end of the 19th century, the British government had given loans to Irish tenant farmers, to allow them to buy the land they worked which was owned by absentee British landlords. The farmers had agreed to pay back a fixed sum of money each year until the loans were repaid. These repayments were called land annuities. When the British left Ireland in 1922, the Free State government agreed to collect the land annuities and transfer the money to Britain. On taking office in 1932, de Valera continued to collect the land annuities from the Irish farmers but refused to send the money to Britain.

The economic war

The British government decided to get the money it was owed by placing a 20% duty on Irish imports. The Irish retaliated by putting taxes on goods coming into the Free State from Britain. De Valera viewed the economic

SOURCE A

Reaction of the British government to the refusal to pay land annuities

The Irish Free State government propose to retain the land annuities .... The Free State government is bound to continue to pay .... and failure to do so would break an agreement which is binding in law.

British Dominion Secretary, in Irish Political Documents, 1916–1949

SOURCE B

A view of the battle over land annuities

If the British government should succeed in beating us in this fight (over land annuities) then we could have no freedom, but at every step they could threaten you .... and force you again to obey the British. What is involved is whether the Irish nation is going to be free or not.

Speech by Eamon de Valera, Fianna Fáil Ard-Fheis, November 1932

Cartoon: The economic war.

war as a chance to make Ireland a self-contained economic unit, hoping that Irish people might respond to the problem of more expensive British goods by setting up their own businesses to compete with British industry.

Although Britain and Northern Ireland's trade with the Free State fell sharply after 1932, Ireland still needed British coal and Britain needed Irish beef and dairy products. Irish farmers were losing millions of pounds because they could find no other market for their produce. As a result, in 1935, the British and Free State governments agreed to lower their respective taxes on coal and beef. The Agreement meant trade and relations between the two countries improved. In 1938, amidst fears of a war in Europe, the British and Irish governments agreed to end their trade dispute. Talks were held in London and, in March 1938, an Anglo-Irish Agreement was signed which brought the economic war to an end.

SOURCE   C

The terms of the Anglo-Irish Agreement 1938

Eire shall:
(a) remove all special taxes placed on British goods sold in Ireland;
(b) pay Britain £10 million as a final settlement of all debts owed to Britain.

Britain shall:
(a) remove all special taxes placed on Irish goods sold in Britain;
(b) leave the naval bases occupied by British troops under the 1921 treaty.

SOURCE   D

Trade between the Free State, Northern Ireland and Great Britain 1932-1938

FREE STATE EXPORTS   FREE STATE IMPORTS

£20,000,000
£50,000,000
£10,000,000
£5,000,000

1932   1934   1936   1938   1932   1934   1936   1938

GREAT BRITAIN   NORTHERN IRELAND

SOURCE E

The north's view of the motives behind the economic war

Between 1924 and 1931 north–south trade was little affected by the border. After 1932 the picture was rapidly altered. De Valera's confrontation policy with Britain from 1932 on, centred on the withholding of land annuities and the tariff war .... was seen in the north as a strategy to destroy the treaty settlement and reopen the question of unity.

D Kennedy, *The Widening Gulf: Northern Attitudes to the Independent Irish State 1919–49*, 1988, with the permission of The Blackstaff Press Ltd

Newspaper announces end of economic war.

SOURCE F

Experience of Donegal farmers during the economic war

The farming community (in Donegal) is passing through most difficult times. Their market towns .... are Londonderry and Strabane. They are now completely cut off from these towns by the boundary and high tariffs .... They have no market in which to sell their cattle or produce and .... can see nothing in the future but black ruin.

Belfast Newsletter, 5 June 1934

THE ECONOMIC WAR IS ENDED

Ireland to Take Over Coast Defence Stations

BRITAIN TO GET £10,000,000 IN FINAL SETTLEMENT

ACTIVITIES

1 Using Sources A and B (page 67) explain why Britain felt the Free State should continue to pay the land annuities and de Valera's reasons for refusing to pay.

2 Using Source C, identify the major territorial concession which Ireland gained from the Anglo-Irish Agreement of 1938.

Use Source D to identify the immediate consequences of the economic war.

3 Use the information in Sources D, E and F to explain how relations between Northern Ireland and the Free State were affected by the economic war. You should mention:

(a) attitudes in Northern Ireland towards the Free State;

(b) the effects of the duties on the border communities;

(c) trade between the two countries.

4 For what reasons did the British and Irish decide to bring the economic war to an end?

5 In what ways did each country benefit from the Anglo-Irish Agreement of 1938?

Return of the Treaty Ports 1938

3.5

Focus

Why did Britain agree to hand over the treaty ports?

What were the reactions to Britain's decision to do this?

The **Anglo-Irish Treaty of 1921** gave Britain the right to maintain garrisons at the ports of Berehaven, Cobh and Lough Swilly because it was thought they could be of great strategic importance to Britain. These three bases became known as the treaty ports. In 1938, as part of the settlement to end the economic war, Britain agreed to return the treaty ports to Ireland. Britain's decision to hand back the ports came as a surprise to most people and caused strong reactions in both Britain and Ireland.

Improved Anglo-Irish relations

In 1938, the growing strength of Germany and its expansionist policy worried most European countries. The British knew the potential value of the treaty ports in a time of war but Neville Chamberlain, the British Prime Minister, felt Britain had more to gain by winning Eire's friendship through returning the ports than by trying to use the ports against the wishes of the Irish. He argued that Eire relied on the British navy for protection and, in a time of emergency, would recognise it was in her own interests to give Britain the use of the ports.

De Valera's view was that Britain's control of the treaty ports made it impossible for Eire to follow an independent foreign policy. He was afraid that Britain would use the ports to involve Eire in any war it was fighting. He felt the return of the treaty ports gave Eire the freedom to decide its own foreign policy and bring an end to British interference in Eire's affairs. As the possibility of war with Germany increased, the British government sought to secure Irish goodwill by agreeing to give back the treaty ports as part of the settlement to end the economic war. Politicians in Britain and Northern Ireland warned that once British forces left Ireland it was unlikely the Irish government would allow them to return.

SOURCE B

Government view of the importance of good relations with Ireland

We came to the conclusion that a friendly Ireland was worth far more to us both in peace and in war than those paper rights that could only be exercised at the risk of maintaining and perhaps increasing their sense of grievance.

Neville Chamberlain, 5 May 1938

SOURCE C

Hope for Irish support in return for the ports

We thought that if we tried to use the ports against the wishes of the Eire government, this might drive Eire into the arms of our enemies. Also we hoped that if there was a war and if – or because – we had given up the ports, Eire could come in on our side.

Malcolm MacDonald, British Dominions Secretary, 1978

SOURCE A

A British view of the declining importance of the ports

The present time seems a suitable one for (returning the treaty ports to Ireland) since the immediate importance of the reserved ports has somewhat decreased in view of the recent change of the defence policy of this country.

British Deputy Chiefs of Staff Report, April 1936

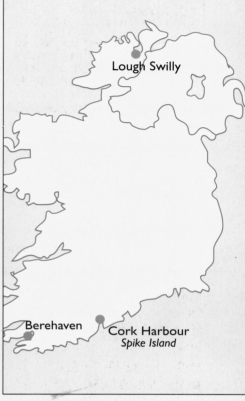

(Above) The location of the treaty ports.

(Above left) British troops prepare to leave Spike Island.

SOURCE D

A change of attitude by Britain towards Ireland

There can be no doubt that British occupation of these ports put great limitations on Irish sovereignty .... The return of the ports to Eire seems to indicate a complete change .... in London. Hitherto the British attitude towards this country has been characterised by a not unnatural suspicion. Now the Admiralty .... has recognised the sincerity of Irish motives, and, has handed over the ports as an act of faith.

The Irish Times, 26 April 1938

SOURCE E

The symbolic importance of the return of the ports

Handing over the treaty ports recognises and finally establishes Irish sovereignty over the 26 counties.

Eamon de Valera, 28 April 1938

SOURCE F

Warning about the strategic importance of the ports

You are casting away real and important means of security .... These ports are in fact the sentinel towers of the western approaches .... Now we are to give them up, unconditionally, to an Irish government led by men .... who have acted against this country .... These ports may be denied us in the hour of need.

Winston Churchill, 5 May 1938

SOURCE G

Unionist warning about the return of the ports

I gave the most solemn warnings to British Ministers on the dangers of such unnecessary action as surrendering these valuable bases for British use as protection not only for Great Britain and Ulster, but for southern Ireland also.

James Craig, 8 November 1940

Winston Churchill.

ACTIVITIES

1   Examine the location of the treaty ports. Why did Britain maintain **garrisons** in these ports after it withdrew from the rest of Ireland in 1922?

2   What reasons are suggested in Sources A, B and C (page 70) for Britain's decision to hand over the treaty ports? Which do you think was the most important reason?

3   Use Sources D and E (page 71) to identify what people in Eire thought was significant about the return of the ports?

4   What were Churchill's views about the return of the treaty ports? (Source F) Winston Churchill had been one of the negotiators of the 1921 Treaty. He believed that de Valera wanted to remove all British influence from Ireland and therefore could not be trusted. Explain how Churchill's views may have been influenced by his previous involvement in Ireland and the changes de Valera had introduced from 1932.

5   Source G was written in 1940, two years after the return of the treaty ports. No evidence exists to prove that Craig warned the British government as he claimed. What do you think Craig hoped to achieve by claiming he had warned Britain about the dangers of returning the treaty ports?

Eire's Neutrality during the
Second World War

Focus

Why did de Valera's government choose to keep Eire neutral during the Second World War?

How did people in Eire feel about neutrality?

On 1 September 1939, Germany invaded Poland. The next day Eire's parliament met in an emergency session and passed laws which gave the government powers to ensure public safety and essential services. In a broadcast to the nation, de Valera announced his intention to adopt a policy of neutrality in order to keep Ireland out of the European war.

Eire at the outbreak of war

During the 1930s, the Irish government had frequently spoken of its commitment to **neutrality** and, as a sign of its independence, most Irish people expected the government to remain neutral when the fighting started. The government felt its duty was to unite the people against outside forces and protect them from the hardships of war. So, when war broke out in 1939, Eire along with 20 other countries, including the United States of America, announced its neutrality.

(Below left) Evening newspaper placards in London announcing the German invasion of Poland.

(Below) The Irish Press announces Eire's neutrality.

IRELAND NEUTRAL

Oireachtas Is Unanimous For Emergency Measures

THE Government intended to pursue its policy of keeping the country out of war, the Taoiseach informed the Oireachtas on Saturday, when a special session of the Dáil and Seanad passed, without division, all stages of the First Amendment of the Constitution Bill and the Emergency Powers Bill. Resolutions were passed declaring a state of national emergency. The Bills were later signed by the President.

Both Houses sat until early yesterday morning to get the measures through. The Seanad adjourned sine die at 4.45 a.m. and the Dáil at 5, until October 18.

Mr. de Valera said that so long as the country, or any part of it, was subject to the application of force by a stronger nation it was only natural that our people, no matter what their sympathies, should look to their own country first, and consider where its interest lay.

Referring to the very serious problems that confronted the Government in the present international situation—neutrality brought problems more difficult than those which arose for belligerents—and to the necessity for the emergency powers, the Taoiseach said: "We know that our power to do this work will depend largely on the amount of public confidence we have ,and the amount to which we are supported by the voluntary co-operation of the people."

"I would like you to realise," he said, "that we may be facing one of the most terrible catastrophes in history—conditions of which we have no knowledge from anything that has happened in the past to foretell what they may be."

Mr. Sean Lemass said that there was no reason for anxiety concerning any of the necessaries of life. He advised against panic buying.

Mr. W. Davin (Lab.) said it was the desire of the overwhelming majority of the people that this country should be kept out of any European conflict. It was satisfactory to know that all parties were lining up behind the Government in that respect.

(Reports of debates on pages 2 and 3.)

GERMANY'S NEUTRALITY ATTITUDE TO IRELAND

MR. DE VALERA intimated to Press representatives while the Dáil was in session yesterday morning that the German Minister had called on him on Thursday last and informed him of Germany's peaceful attitude towards Ireland and said that if Germany were engaged in a European war the German Government would respect Ireland's neutrality, provided it was adhered to.

Mr. de Valera replied that the Irish Government wished to remain at peace with Germany, as with all other Powers, and referred to a statement published in the Press on February 20 last, that the aim of Government policy was to maintain and preserve Ireland's neutrality in the event of war.

GIANT GERMAN LINER CAPTURED

High French quarters state that the British have captured the German liner Bremen at 8 p.m. but the area in which the liner was captured was not mentioned. It was stated that she had been taken to a British port, but the British Ministry of Information announced last night that the Admiralty knew nothing about the capture of the Bremen.

TIDE TIMES
FOR BATHERS
High Water at Dublin.

	Mrg. Aftn.
To-day	.8 4 3.15
To-morrow	.3 59 4.54
Wednesday	.4 25 4.60

HIGH WATER

	Mrg. Aftn.		Mrg. Aftn.
Ballina	9.51 10.11	Galway	9 6 9.26
Belfast	2.34 2.55	Limerick	10.38 10.55
Cobh	9.11 9.30	Sligo	9.21 10. 9
Cork	9.14 9.33	Westport	9.21 9.41
Derry	6. 7 6.29	Waterford	10.12 10.51
Drogheda	2.52 2.21	Youghal	9.16 9.35
Dundalk	1.40 6. 0	

Lighting-up Time, 9.16 p.m.

Dixon and Hempenstall. Barometer and Thermometers. 111 Lower Grafton Street (between Suffolk Street and College Green). (Advt.)

MINISTERS TAKE OVER NEW DUTIES

THE Taoiseach announced last night a reorganisation of the Government as follows: —

Minister for Supplies—Sean Lemass. Minister for Co-Ordination of Military and Civil Defence — Mr. Frank Aiken.

Minister for Industry and Commerce—Tomas O Deirg. Minister for Defence—Mr. Oscar Traynor.

Minister for Lands and Posts and Telegraphs—Mr. Gerald Boland. Ministry of Local Government and Ministry of Education — The Tanaiste.

THE Taoiseach, Mr. de Valera, in a broadcast address to the nation from Radio-Eireann last night, said:

"I am speaking to you to-night because I thought you would expect me to. I have been too busy to prepare any connected manuscript, so I must speak to you from notes. I know you will understand. You know from the News bulletins to which you have been listening that the great European powers are again at war. That war would be the end has appeared almost inevitable for months past. Such escape as we had a year ago could hardly be expected to occur twice, until a short time ago there was no hope is gone and the peoples of Europe are plunged once more into misery and anguish of war.

AIM—KEEP OUT OF WAR.

"Noting the march of events, the Government decided its policy last spring and announced its decision to you and to the world. We resolved that the aim of our policy would [be to] keep our people out of a war," said in the Dáil, with... with our experience and with a part of... unjustly severed fr[om]... no other decision... was possible.

"That we were right is proved by the acceptance by the people of our policy since it was announced to them. Not a single member of the Dáil or Senate suggested during the long sessions yesterday or this morning that there was any other policy that could be adopted. I know that, no matter what might be the views of any section of our people on the merits of the present dispute—the dispute which has occasioned this conflict—there is no difference of opinion amongst them...

...[y] st... ...policy... ...felt that... ...other policy...

(Continued on Page 8)

Neutrality was made possible by the return of the treaty ports in 1938. Some people saw neutrality as a chance to show Eire's independence from Britain. However, neutrality did not guarantee Eire's security. Eire was not equipped to fight a war. Its armed forces were limited and it relied on Britain to protect ships bringing cargo to Irish ports. In the five months between April and August 1940, the Axis powers (Germany and Italy) occupied eight neutral countries in Europe. On several occasions, the British government tried to persuade Eire to join the struggle against Germany but de Valera declined.

Irish views of neutrality

Most people in Eire agreed with the government's policy of neutrality but sympathised with the Allied cause. Forty thousand of them joined the British armed forces during the war and between 150,000 and 180,000 people from Eire worked in support of the war effort. A small number of people felt Eire should abandon neutrality and join the Allies in the fight against Germany. This view became more popular after 1941, when the United States joined the Allies, but it never had widespread support and was strongly resisted by de Valera's government. Eire's neutrality caused resentment among Protestants in Northern Ireland.

SOURCE A

British cartoon image of Irish neutrality

The Daily Mail, 1940.

SOURCE B

Views on neutrality

All the small states can do, if the statesmen of greater states fail in their duties (to prevent war), is to decide that they will not become the tools of any great power, and they will resist .... every attempt to force them into war against their will.

Eamon de Valera, Geneva, 1936

SOURCE C

Reasons for neutrality

(The government) stands before you as the guardians of the interests of our people, and it is to guard these interests as best we can that we are proposing to follow the policy (of neutrality).

Eamon de Valera, Dáil, 2 September 1939

SOURCE D

Support for neutrality in Eire

Irish neutrality had widespread support. The political parties, the churches, the media, even Irishmen in British uniforms supported Irish neutrality .... Any movement from neutrality by de Valera would have split his cabinet, his party, the parliament, public opinion and could have led to a civil war.

P Taylor, Atlantic Bridgehead, BBC 1991

A shoe shop in Birmingham damaged by an IRA bomb, February 1940.

The IRA and the war

The **IRA** viewed the war as a chance to remove all British influence from Ireland, to end partition and create of a 32 county Irish Republic. The IRA had contacts with Germany during the war but received little practical help from the German government. IRA attempts to assist German agents in Ireland, and to disrupt the British war effort, were mainly unsuccessful.

The Irish government feared Britain might use the activities of the IRA as an excuse to invade Eire. The government took a firm stand against the IRA and allowed two hunger strikers to die in 1940 rather than give in to their demands for political status and, in 1940, de Valera introduced the Emergency Powers (Amendment) Act which gave the government the power to **intern** people without trial.

SOURCE   E

Eire's defences

At the outbreak of the Second World War .... the composition of (Eire's) Defence Forces were as follows:

- *regulars – 630 officers, 1,412 non-commissioned officers, and 5,452 privates;*

- *the A and B reservists – 194 officers, 544 non-commissioned officers, and 4,328 privates;*

- *volunteers – 327 officers, 557 non-commissioned officers, and 6,429 privates;*

- *no navy;*

- *a small airforce;*

- *a total of less than 20,000 in the armed forces.*

T C Salmon, *Unneutral Ireland*, 1989, with the permission of Oxford University Press

SOURCE   F

What if Britain is defeated?

If Britain is beaten in this war through lack of assistance that Ireland might give or get from her, we will have no self-esteem left as a nation.

General Richard Mulcahy, 1939

SOURCE   G

The symbolism of neutrality

Our neutrality towards other nations is not the declaration of an unfriendly intent but the statement of a natural right .... It is our practical claim to independence.

The Bell, 1939

SOURCE   H

Support for neutrality

It is remarkable how even the pro-British group, men who have fought for the Crown and are anxious to be called up again, men whose sons are at the front today .... agree generally in supporting the policy of neutrality for Eire. They see no possible alternative.

John Maffey, British Representative to Ireland, 1939

ACTIVITIES

1 What is the cartoonist's prediction in Source A (page 74) of what will become of Eire as a result of its neutrality. Why might this cartoon have been published in an English newspaper in November 1940?

2 Use Sources B to E (pages 74-76) to identify the social, political and military reasons for Ireland's policy of neutrality.

3 Using Sources G and H, explain why the view expressed by Mulcahy in Source F was generally not shared by his fellow countrymen.

4 Using all the information in this section, explain why Eire's government decided to remain neutral at the outbreak of the Second World War. In your answer you should consider:

(a) problems facing the government in Eire in 1939;

(b) attitudes of Eire's population;

(c) Eire's military strength;

(d) the political importance of neutrality.

War Bargaining: Ulster as a Pawn

Focus

Why did the British government make an offer to end partition?

Why was the offer refused?

Eire's decision to remain neutral meant that Northern Ireland was of even greater strategic importance in keeping the economic lifeline between Britain and the United States open. When Britain declared war on Germany on 3 September 1939 the Northern Ireland government immediately pledged its support for the British war effort. Many people in Northern Ireland volunteered for the British armed forces and worked in agriculture and industry to help the war effort. In June 1940, however, the British government sent proposals to the Eire government suggesting an end to partition.

The situation in 1940

Since its formation in 1921, Northern Ireland's foreign policy was controlled by Britain, so Northern Ireland automatically became involved in the conflict. In 1940 the war was going badly for Britain. Between April and June 1940 German forces invaded and captured Denmark, Norway, Holland, Belgium, Luxembourg and France. Britain now stood alone against the might of Germany. In this dark hour the British government tried to persuade Eire to abandon neutrality and help Britain in its life-or-death struggle.

SOURCE A

A United Ireland in principle

There should be a declaration of a United Ireland in principle .... Ulster to remain involved in the war, Eire to remain neutral .... for the time being; .... a Joint Defence Council to be set up at once .... British naval ships to be allowed into Eire's ports, British troops and aeroplanes to be stationed at certain agreed points in the territory, the British government to provide additional equipment for Eire's forces.

British proposal to the government of Eire by Malcolm MacDonald, 21 June 1940

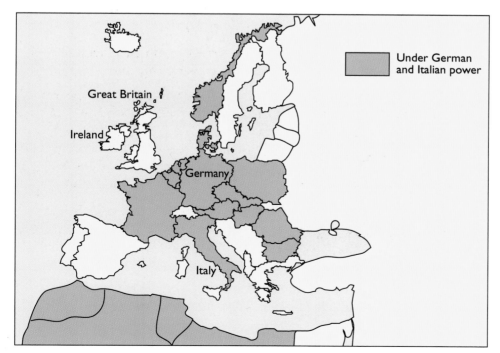

Map of conquered Europe, 1940.

Britain's offer to end partition

In June 1940 Britain's Minister of Health, Malcolm MacDonald, went to Dublin to try to get Eire to join Britain in the war. The British government hoped its promise to end **partition** would persuade Eire to end its neutrality. Neville Chamberlain, Britain's Prime Minister until May 1940, did not discuss the offer to end partition with the Northern Ireland government. He said he *did not believe the Ulster government would refuse to play its part* in bringing Eire into the war, even if it meant having to accept the end of partition.

But de Valera treated the offer with caution. He wanted to know how the British government was going to get the people of Northern Ireland to accept a united Ireland. According to the historian J Bowman, he was also unhappy at the thought of the consequences for Ireland of Ulster Protestants being pushed into a united Ireland against their will. He decided Eire's neutrality should not be given up for a promise which might conveniently be forgotten once the danger to Britain had passed.

Lord Craigavon.

SOURCE B

Unionist reaction

AM PROFOUNDLY SHOCKED AND DISGUSTED BY YOUR LETTER MAKING SUGGESTIONS SO FAR-REACHING BEHIND MY BACK AND WITHOUT ANY PRECONSULTATION WITH ME. TO SUCH TREACHERY TO LOYAL ULSTER I WILL NEVER BE A PARTY.

Lord Craigavon, to the British government, 27 June 1940

SOURCE C

De Valera says no to British plan

We are unable to accept the plan outlined, which we note .... has not been submitted to Lord Craigavon and his colleagues .... The plan would commit us definitely to an immediate abandonment of neutrality. On the other hand it gives no guarantee that in the end we would have a united Ireland, unless indeed concession were made to Lord Craigavon against the wishes and desires of the great majority of the Irish people.

De Valera, to British government, 5 July 1940

ACTIVITIES

1 How did Britain's attitude to Northern Ireland change when war broke out in 1939?

2 Why was Britain willing to consider ending the partition of Ireland in June 1940?

3 Look at Sources A, B and C (pages 77-78).
   (a) How did Britain try to get Eire to abandon its neutrality?
   (b) Why was Craig 'shocked and disgusted' by the British offer to Eire?
   (c) Why do you think de Valera refused Britain's offer to end partition?

4 Britain's offer to end partition created strong reactions in Northern Ireland. How might the following people have felt about Britain's offer:
   (a) an Ulster unionist;
   (b) a nationalist in Northern Ireland.

Relationships during the War

> ### *Focus*
>
> ### *How did the war affect relations among Britain, Northern Ireland and Eire?*

*The war brought Britain and Northern Ireland closer together. People felt their shared experiences of **rationing**, **blackouts**, bombings and loss of loved ones, united them and emphasised how different Britain and Northern Ireland were from Eire.*

Northern Ireland's contribution to the war

Between 1939 and 1945 the people of Northern Ireland worked to help Britain in the struggle against Germany. During the war:

- 40,000 men and women from Northern Ireland fought with the British armed forces;

- Harland and Wolff converted over 3,000 vessels into warships and built 170 new warships;

- Short Brothers and Harland was described as the *finest seaplane manufacturing base in the British Isles;*

The Belfast built Short Sunderland flying boat, which played a big role in the war against U-boats.

- James Mackie and Sons supplied large numbers of anti-aircraft shells;

- the linen mills and shirt factories produced uniforms, overalls and parachutes;

- many farmers changed from **livestock farming** to cereal production to provide additional food for the war effort;

- Northern Ireland's ports provided bases for ships protecting the north Atlantic convoys;

- from January 1942, Northern Ireland was used to provide training bases for American forces. By the end of 1943, there were 100,000 American servicemen in Northern Ireland.

SOURCE A

Eire sends aid to the North at the time of the Blitz

STOP PRESS

It was confirmed in Dublin this morning that units of fire fighting and ambulance services from some towns in Eire assisted to put out fires resulting from Northern Ireland's blitz.

Northern Whig, April 1941

SOURCE B

The extent of Northern Ireland's part in the war

The unionist government tried desperately to be fully included in wartime activities and experiences occurring elsewhere in the United Kingdom .... (but) the British government was not willing to accept Ulster as a full partner in the war .... Throughout the war major strategic decisions about the use of Northern Irish ports and land facilities were made without consultation with the Stormont government.

D Harman, *Education and Enmity: The Control of Schooling in Northern Ireland*, 1973, with the permission of the Institute of Irish Studies, Queen's University, Belfast

Attitudes to Eire

The outbreak of the war increased tension between Northern Ireland and Eire. Many people in Northern Ireland saw Eire's failure to join the war as an act of betrayal and a threat to British security. De Valera was criticised for allowing the German Minister to remain in Ireland and there were widespread rumours of German spies living in Eire.

Relations between north and south improved for a short period in 1941, after Eire sent fire engines across the border to help Belfast deal with the fires and devastation caused by the German bombing raid. But the improved relations did not last long and de Valera's protests, in 1942, about American forces being based in Northern Ireland were taken as proof of his pro-German sympathies. At the end of the war, de Valera's visit to Hempel, the German Minister to Ireland, to express his condolences on the death of **Hitler**, caused resentment in Britain and Northern Ireland.

Finishing 20mm Hurricane cannon shells at Mackies, 1941.

SOURCE C

The strategic importance of Northern Ireland

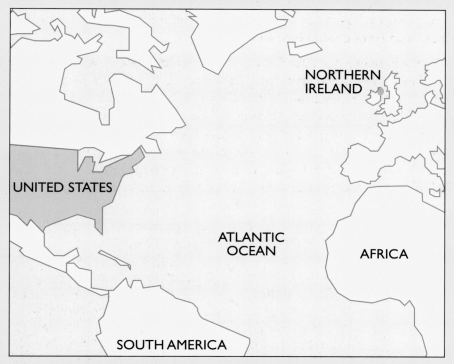

NORTHERN IRELAND

UNITED STATES

ATLANTIC OCEAN

AFRICA

SOUTH AMERICA

Northern Ireland plays a key role in the Battle of the Atlantic .... Her strategic position alone ensures that her contribution is a crucial one. The unprotected gap in the mid-Atlantic .... would have been far wider if it had not been for the coastal command bases in Northern Ireland.

Herbert Morrison, British Home Secretary, 10 July 1943

ACTIVITIES

1 With reference to the illustration on page 80, describe the contribution Northern Ireland made to the war effort.

2 Describe the standpoint of Eire towards:
   (a) Britain and
   (b) Northern Ireland during the war.

3 Use the illustration on page 80 and Sources B to D to explain how and why Britain's attitude towards Northern Ireland changed during the war. Give reasons for these changes.

4 What do Sources D and E suggest about Britain's relations with Eire at the end of the war?

SOURCE D

The significance of Northern Ireland's part in the war

Owing to the action of Mr de Valera .... the approaches which the southern Irish ports and airfields could so easily have guarded were closed by hostile aircraft and U-boats. This was indeed a deadly moment in our life, and had it not been for the loyalty and friendship of Northern Ireland, we should have been forced to come to close quarters with Mr de Valera, or perish forever from the earth.

Winston Churchill, 13 May 1945

SOURCE E

Response to Churchill

Mr Churchill makes it clear that, in certain circumstances, he would have violated our neutrality and he would have justified his action by Britain's necessity .... Mr Churchill is proud of Britain's stand alone, after France had fallen and before America entered the war. Could he not find in his heart the generosity to acknowledge that there is a small nation (Ireland) that stood alone, not for one year or two, but for several hundred years against aggression; a small nation that could never be got to accept defeat and has never surrendered her soul?

De Valera, radio broadcast, 17 May 1945

An Era of Change: A Labour Government

3.9

Focus

How did the coming to power of a Labour government in 1945 affect relations between Britain and Northern Ireland?

The war brought prosperity to Northern Ireland and forged closer links with Britain. Immediately after the war, Ulster **Unionists** considered the union and their relationship with Britain to be more secure than ever. As supporters of the Conservative Party at Westminster, however, their sense of security was shattered when the Labour Party won the British general election in 1945. The Labour Party was known to oppose partition and Ulster Unionists feared the new British Prime Minister, Clement Attlee, might try to force the six counties into a united Ireland.

Labour government attitude towards Stormont

Members of the new Labour government questioned the ability and fairness of the Stormont government. Between 1945 and 1951, relations between Attlee's Labour government and Stormont were tense. Nevertheless, Northern Ireland faired well under Labour, which introduced a **welfare state** to improve living conditions for everyone in Britain and Northern Ireland. Disputes between the two governments were usually settled in Northern Ireland's favour.

SOURCE A

Attlee feeding Basil Brooke a socialist medicine he does not like

ACTIVITIES

1 Use Sources A to D to list the reasons why the Stormont government was worried about having a Labour government at Westminster.

2 What insights does Source A provide into the Northern Ireland government's expected reaction to the introduction of the welfare state?

SOURCE B

Labour view of the Northern Ireland Cabinet

*Remnants of the old **ascendancy class**, very frightened of Catholics and the general world trend to the left (socialism).*

Chuter Ede, the British Home Secretary in 1946

SOURCE C

Unionist suspicion of the motives of the new Labour government

It may be part of Labour policy to create conditions whereby we (in Northern Ireland) might be forced into the Free State.

Basil Brooke, Prime Minister of Northern Ireland, 9 October 1945

SOURCE D

Unionist suspicion of the possible impact of Labour's policies

There were fears at Stormont that a clash .... (with Westminster) would eventually occur .... caused .... by the nature of the social and economic policies being introduced by Attlee and his colleagues .... What concerned several members of the Unionist Cabinet most was .... (that) an expansion of central government would inevitably whittle away the .... power of Stormont.

Brian Maginess, Stormont Minister, 5 February 1946

The Declaration of a Republic:
A Threat to the North?

> ### Focus
>
> **What was the reaction to Eire's decision to become a Republic in 1948?**
>
> **What effect did the decision have on Eire's relations with Northern Ireland and Britain?**

*In September 1948, John A Costello, the leader of the new **coalition** government which defeated de Valera in the 1948 elections, announced his intention to leave the British Commonwealth and to make Eire a Republic. These decisions caused concern at Westminster and Stormont. While Britain wondered how Eire's decisions would affect the Commonwealth there were fears in Northern Ireland that, in becoming a Republic, Eire was taking a step towards a united Ireland.*

The Anti-Partition League

Unionists were concerned when a group of Northern Ireland nationalists opposed to partition formed the Anti-Partition League in 1945. This League grew rapidly and received support from Eire and Irish communities in Britain and America. League members were unhappy with de Valera's policy that silence about the north was the best way to make progress on partition. Eire's coalition government's offer to give unionists *any reasonable constitutional guarantees* they desired if they agreed to reunification delighted

---

SOURCE

Cartoon

SIR BASIL: "DEV COULDN'T CRACK IT, SO YOU'D BETTER GIVE UP THE BIG IDEA."

The Voice of Ulster, March 1948, Vol I No 6

SOURCE B

Unionist view

The Republic is a political manoeuvre .... Ulster will need to be vigilant, virile and valiant. All parties are after its prosperous industries and its energetic and thrifty people. Evidently they assume that .... the declaration of Easter Monday will blow the Border away.

The Voice of Ulster, April/May 1949

the League members, even though Brooke dismissed the offer saying that *Ulster is not for sale.*

Unionists seek further guarantees from Westminster

Sir Basil Brooke, the Northern Ireland Prime Minister, went to England to explain Ulster unionists' fears and to get assurance from the British government that Northern Ireland would not be abandoned. Attlee promised that Northern Ireland's position in the United Kingdom was secure.

The 1949 'chapel gate elections'

Brooke called an election for February 1949 to give the people of Northern Ireland a chance to show their support for the union. The Anti-Partition League asked Eire for help to fight the elections in Northern Ireland in February 1949. Politicians in Eire agreed a collection should be organised to help finance anti-partition candidates in the election. *The Belfast Telegraph* called the collections, 'the chapel gate collections' and the election itself was promptly nicknamed 'the chapel gate election'. Unionists were annoyed by Eire's attempt to interfere in Northern Ireland's affairs and there were many bitter sectarian clashes during the election campaign. Although unionists won 40 of the 52 seats at Stormont, due partly to their continued majority within the state, nevertheless, they continued to feel insecure.

Sir Basil Brooke meeting Clement Attlee, August 1948.

Ulster holds the Fort !

Maintain our Freedom

VOTE UNIONIST

Unionist poster.

The constitutional status of Northern Ireland guaranteed

In June 1949, after the 26 counties officially became the Republic of Ireland, the government at Westminster was persuaded to pass the Government of Ireland Act which gave Stormont the power to decide when Northern Ireland's position in the United Kingdom would change. In 1951, the Anti-Partition League ceased to be active, partly because of its candidates' poor performance in the 1949 election, and partly because of a general lack of interest in partition on both sides of the border.

SOURCE

Republic's reaction to constitutional guarantees for Northern Ireland, an historian's view

Following upon the declaration of the Republic, Mr Costello's government promoted a campaign to attract more attention to the seeming injustice of the division of Ireland. This was partly in response to the decision of Mr Attlee's Labour administration to introduce by Act of Parliament a guarantee that no change should be made regarding the constitutional connection between Northern Ireland and Britain without the consent of the former .... The anti-partition committee was active for a number of years without results.

T D Williams, Conclusion, in K Nowlan and T D Williams (eds), *Ireland in the War Years and After,* 1969, with the permission of Gill and Macmillan Ltd

SOURCE

British Labour government view

The United Kingdom government will not regard .... Eire in the category of foreign countries or Eire citizens in the category of foreigners.

Clement Attlee, in House of Commons, 25 November 1948

SOURCE

The Union strengthened

In no event will Northern Ireland or any part thereof cease to be part .... of the United Kingdom without the consent of the parliament of Northern Ireland.

Government of Ireland Act 1949

ACTIVITIES

1 The cartoon (Source A, page 83) gives a unionist reaction to the election of the coalition government in Eire. According to the cartoon, what is Northern Ireland's attitude to Eire's new coalition government?

2 Use Sources B, C and D to explain how Eire's decision to become a Republic affected Britain's relations with:
 (a) Eire; and
 (b) Northern Ireland.

3 Study Source E. How and why did Costello react to the Government of Ireland Act 1949?

4 Write a letter from a member of the Anti-Partition League to a friend explaining:
 (a) why the Anti-Partition League was formed;
 (b) why the Anti-Partition League candidates won so few seats in the 1949 elections;
 (c) why the Anti-Partition League stopped its activities.

The Welfare State

3.11

Focus

What changes did the post-war Labour government introduce, what did they involve and what effect did they have on Northern Ireland?

The post-war Labour government which came to power in Britain introduced great changes in the way the country was run, including nationalising major industries and setting up a welfare state and national health service.

The welfare state and nationalisation

The welfare state was the name given to the government plan to set up and pay for a system of care and benefits for everyone who needed it 'from the cradle to the grave'. From 1944 onwards, the government passed various Acts of Parliament setting up: in 1944, free secondary education for all; in 1945 family allowance payments for children; in 1946 a free national health service and unemployment benefit without means testing; and in 1948 national assistance payments for the needy. The Labour government also **nationalised** key industries, bringing them under State ownership and control. Between 1946 and 1949, the Bank of England, the coal mines, air transport, electricity, railways and roads, gas, iron and steel were all nationalised.

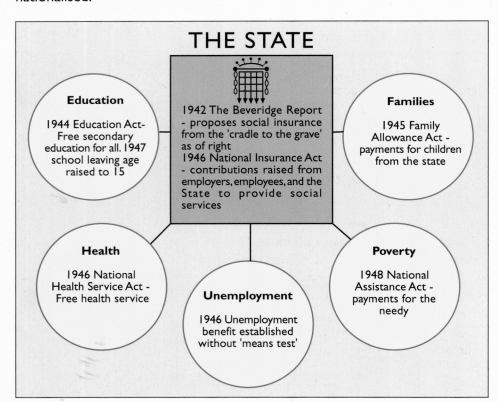

THE STATE

Education
1944 Education Act- Free secondary education for all. 1947 school leaving age raised to 15

1942 The Beveridge Report - proposes social insurance from the 'cradle to the grave' as of right
1946 National Insurance Act - contributions raised from employers, employees, and the State to provide social services

Families
1945 Family Allowance Act - payments for children from the state

Health
1946 National Health Service Act - Free health service

Unemployment
1946 Unemployment benefit established without 'means test'

Poverty
1948 National Assistance Act - payments for the needy

SOCIALISM LEADS TO COMMUNISM

VOTE UNIONIST

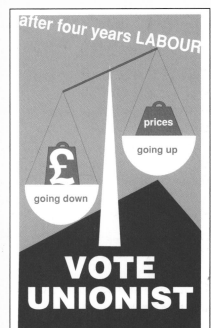

after four years LABOUR

prices going up

£ going down

VOTE UNIONIST

(Above) Unionist election literature.

The founding of the welfare state.

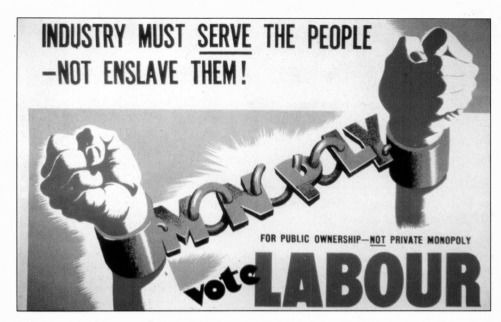

Labour election poster 'Industry must serve the people'.

The welfare state in Northern Ireland

The Unionist government of Northern Ireland was very conservative and was not in favour of such rapid change. Unionists, who had strong links with the British Conservative Party, did not want to be linked to Labour's socialist policies. Many unionist politicians were businessmen and did not agree with nationalisation and the creation of the welfare state. Some considered making Northern Ireland a separate country in the British Commonwealth to avoid having to introduce the welfare state and nationalisation. Only after the British government arranged to pay for the cost of the welfare state in Northern Ireland did the Unionist government agree, reluctantly, to introduce the changes. This made the Northern Ireland government even more dependent on finance from Westminster.

Changes after 1945 in housing, health, social services and education

In 1945, the Northern Ireland Housing Trust was set up to build 100,000 new houses. Local councils were also encouraged to build more houses. In 1948 the Health Services Act set up the national health service in Northern Ireland. Between 1945 and 1950, unemployment benefit, pensions, family allowance and health insurance schemes were introduced at British rates of payment. In 1947, the Education Act introduced a modern system of primary education for children up to the age of 11, followed by either secondary or grammar school up to the age of 15. An end to religious instruction in schools was also proposed.

Farming and industry

Farming had expanded during the war and now was using modern methods and machinery. This continued after 1947 when the British government guaranteed food prices and markets by the 1947 Agriculture Act. The Industries Development Act of 1944 offered grants, factory premises and equipment to attract new industries. This gave Northern Ireland more advantages than many parts of Britain.

Results

HOUSING	• The Housing Trust built houses for those who could afford the rents. Building 100,000 homes took almost 20 years. Trust houses were allocated fairly. • Local councils did not build enough houses. Council houses were not given out fairly, especially to Catholics.
HEALTH	• Hospitals were better organised. • Free medical services became available for all citizens. • Health standards improved.
BENEFITS	• The Poor Law and Boards of Guardians were abolished. • All citizens had the same benefit payments as in the rest of the United Kingdom. • Northern Ireland citizens were generally better off than those in the Republic.
EDUCATION	• Catholic and Protestant churches demanded separate schools. • The 11+ exam made grammar schools available to all children. • Secondary school pupil numbers doubled by 1952. • Grants to students helped more young people to go to university.
INDUSTRY	• By 1946 ten new factories opened promising to create 4,710 new jobs. • 75% of new factories opened up to 1963 were based around Belfast. • Only 16 out of 111 new factories were built in Counties Londonderry, Tyrone and Fermanagh. • Unemployment remained high compared with other parts of Britain.
FARMING	• Government grants and rising food prices made farmers prosperous. • Modern methods led to unemployment for many farm workers.

ACTIVITIES

1 *What changes were brought about by the Labour government in Britain after 1945?*

2 *Why do you think a large number of unionists were opposed to the Labour government changes?*

The Decline of the IRA

Focus

Why did the desire of nationalists for a United Ireland recede during the 1950s?

The return of a Conservative government at Westminster in 1951 allowed Stormont politicians to rule Northern Ireland without interference from Britain. Social and economic developments in Northern Ireland as a result of the welfare state widened the gap between living standards in Northern Ireland and the Republic during the 1950s.

Decline of republicanism in the north

The Northern Ireland government welcomed the return of their Conservative allies to power in 1951. The Conservative government took little interest in Northern Ireland, content to let Stormont look after its

SOURCE B

Unionist government view of the situation in Northern Ireland

The man in the street is well pleased with the present position. Our economic status has not been affected by socialist legislation .... We are doing rightly at the moment .... The two main parties (in Britain are) not unfriendly .... We are weakening the anti-partition movement which is fading visibly.

Brian Maginess, Northern Ireland Minister of Labour and National Insurance, 5 August 1951

SOURCE A

Cartoon

'The Baby Sitter'

SOURCE C

The effect of the welfare state upon Catholics

Compulsory national insurance, increased family allowances and the health service all helped to shield Catholics from the worst effects of unemployment and poverty .... and since such were not available south of the border the tendency to regard the achievement of a united Ireland as the only way to make things better began to weaken. The overall effect on the Northern Ireland Catholics of post-war change was a lessening urgency about the border coupled with a growing impatience about discrimination.

E McCann, *War and an Irish Town*, 1974

own affairs. The 1950s and early 1960s were a time of prosperity for Northern Ireland when most people enjoyed a rise in living standards. An IRA campaign, between 1956 and 1962, was abandoned through lack of support, suggesting that nationalists had lost interest in achieving a united Ireland.

SOURCE D

The effect of the welfare state upon partition

The welfare state reinforced partition by opening up a wide gap with the south .... the plain truth was that Northern Ireland enjoyed a high level of services and benefits because its position in the United Kingdom provided it with massive finances. Without British help, life in Northern Ireland would have been very different.

P Buckland, *A History of Northern Ireland*, 1981, with the permission of Gill and Macmillan Ltd (adapted)

SOURCE E

Unemployment and emigration from the Republic

The 1950s was the dark hour of nationalist Ireland .... Between 1950 and 1959 there were fewer jobs available and cross-channel boats ferried the youth of the Republic to find work in Britain at the rate of 40,000 emigrants annually.

L Kennedy, *The Modern Industrialisation of Ireland 1940–1988*, 1989, with the permission of the Economic and Social History Society of Ireland

SOURCE F

Cartoon

ILL-PAID EIRE WORKER: "WOULDN'T I JUST LIKE TO LIVE IN THAT SAME 'BLACK' NORTH!"

The Voice of Ulster, January 1948, Vol I No 4

SOURCE G

The focus of the IRA campaign 1956–1962

The IRA campaign in Northern Ireland launched in December 1956, concentrated on police and military targets in the border areas .... The deaths in the entire campaign totalled 19. Internment without trial was used .... against the IRA both north and south of the Border.

R Fanning, Independent Ireland, 1983

SOURCE H

End of the IRA campaign

The decision to end the resistance campaign has been taken in view of the general situation. Foremost among the facts motivating this course of action has been the attitude of the general public whose minds have been deliberately distracted from the supreme issues facing the Irish people – the unity of and freedom of Ireland.

IRA statement, 1962

The customs post at Strabane, Co. Tyrone after a bomb explosion in 1957.

ACTIVITIES

1   Look closely at Source A (page 89). What is the cartoonist's view of Britain's attitude towards Northern Ireland?

2   What reasons are suggested in Sources B to F (pages 89–90) to explain why the support among Northern Catholics for a united Ireland weakened during the 1950s?

3   According to Sources E and F, how healthy was the economy of the Republic in the early 1950s?

4   Source F is taken from the front cover of a unionist magazine. In what ways might this affect the viewpoint put forward?

5   In what ways is Source F supported or unsupported by Source E. Use details from both sources to support your answer.

6   Use all the sources in this section to explain why the IRA campaign of 1956–62 failed.

Part 4
THE CAUSES AND CONSEQUENCES OF POLITICAL UNREST WITHIN NORTHERN IRELAND

TIMELINE

DATE

1963	Captain Terence O'Neill becomes Prime Minister of Northern Ireland.
1965	O'Neill meets with Taoiseach Sean Lemass.
1967	O'Neill meets with Taoiseach Jack Lynch. The Civil Rights Association is formed.
1968	The mass civil rights campaign begins.
1969	O'Neill resigns, civil disturbances continue. British troops are sent in. The IRA is revived.
1970	Provisional IRA is formed. The Alliance Party and the Social Democratic and Labour Party (SDLP) are formed.
1971	The Ulster Volunteer Force (UVF) revives.
1971–76	Internment is introduced.
1972	Bloody Sunday. Stormont falls and direct rule is imposed.
1973	The Sunningdale Agreement is signed.
1974	The Power-sharing Executive begins to govern. The Ulster Workers' Council calls a strike. The Power-sharing Executive falls.
1976	The Peace People are formed.
1977–80	The 'blanket' and 'dirty' protests begin.
1980–81	The hunger strike campaigns end in the death of ten hunger strikers.
1983	The New Ireland Forum meets.
1984	The IRA bombs the Conservative Party conference at Brighton.
1985	The Anglo-Irish Agreement is signed.
1985–87	'Ulster Says No' Campaign gets under way.
1993	The Downing Street Declaration is agreed.
1994	IRA calls a cessation of military operations. Loyalists call a ceasefire. Ban on Sinn Féin is lifted. Beginning of official talks with Sinn Féin.

Building Bridges Between the Two Traditions

4.1

Focus

What actions did Terence O'Neill take in pursuit of his three aims?

In 1963, Captain Terence O'Neill replaced Lord Brookeborough as Prime Minister of Northern Ireland. O'Neill wanted to make Northern Ireland economically stronger and prosperous .... and to build bridges between the two traditions within the community. O'Neill adopted a three-pronged policy of economic development, conciliation of the two communities within Northern Ireland and improving relations with the Republic.

Captain O'Neill meeting Sean Lemass, 1965.

O'Neill visiting a Catholic school.

Economic development and community reconciliation

The traditional ship-building and linen industries were declining.

- O'Neill aimed to attract new industries to Northern Ireland by offering them attractive investment grants and tax allowances.

- He tried to improve the attitudes of Protestants to Catholics, and of Catholics to the State, by symbolic gestures such as visiting Catholic dignitaries, schools and other institutions.

- O'Neill promised reforms in housing, education and the voting system.

- He invited the **Taoiseach** of the Republic, Sean Lemass, to Stormont in 1965 for talks on cross-border trade links, the first official visit of its kind since partition.

- O'Neill declared the **Ulster Volunteer Force** an illegal organisation in June 1966 after they claimed responsibility for killing two Catholics.

- He set up a Ministry of Development which built new houses, factories and motorways.

- O'Neill developed a new town, Craigavon, linking Lurgan and Portadown.

- He set up a new university at Coleraine.

Shaking hands across the border

O'Neill also tried to improve relations with the Republic of Ireland. The Republic's economy had started to improve in the 1960s and O'Neill hoped both areas could benefit by developing trade links with each other. In 1965, he invited the Taoiseach, Sean Lemass, to Belfast for talks about cross-border co-operation and trade. Shortly afterwards, O'Neill made a return visit to Dublin, where it was announced that Northern Ireland and the Republic would start to co-operate in tourism and in the provision of electricity supplies.

A public opinion poll taken in Northern Ireland in 1967 suggested that O'Neill had substantial Protestant support and much goodwill among middle-class Catholics.

ACTIVITIES

1 In what ways do the pictorial sources suggest that O'Neill was attempting to build bridges between the two traditions in the Northern Ireland community and to improve relationships with the Republic?

2 What evidence is there to suggest that the economy and society of Northern Ireland was improving under O'Neill?

Opposition to O'Neill

4.2

> ### Focus
>
> **What aspects of O'Neill's policies attracted opposition from both sides of the community?**

O'Neill's policies were not popular with everyone. He was considered too liberal by many within his own party and well meaning, but too slow in taking real action, by a newly emerging younger generation of educated Catholics. His economic policies were believed by Nationalists to be aimed only at increasing the prosperity of the more Protestant areas east of the Bann and neglecting the Catholic areas west of the Bann.

Tensions with fellow Unionists over contact with the Republic

Many **unionists** objected to O'Neill's contacts with the Republic. Many Protestants were deeply distrustful of the southern state particularly because Articles 2 and 3 of the 1937 Constitution *laid claim to the whole of the island of Ireland.*

The idea that Home Rule meant Rome Rule was strengthened in northern Protestant minds by Article 44 of the 1937 Irish Constitution which recognised *the special position of the Roman Catholic Church.* Even though this article recognised *the Church of Ireland, the Presbyterian Church, the Methodist Church, the Society of Friends, the Jewish congregations and the other denominations existing in Ireland,* Protestants in the north generally did not believe the declaration in the Constitution that *the State would not discriminate on the grounds of religious profession, belief or status.*

A number of other matters added to general Protestant suspicion of the Catholic Church and the special position it was given in the southern state:

*   the Catholic Church's controversial '**Ne Temere Decree**' of 1908 did not recognise mixed marriages between Catholics and Protestants if they were not solemnised by the Catholic Church;

*   the same decree required Catholics marrying Protestants to bring up their children as Catholics;

*   divorce or the remarriage of persons divorced elsewhere was forbidden by Article 41 of the 1937 Irish Constitution;

*   the importation and sale of contraceptives was banned by section 17 of the Criminal Law Amendment Act 1935.

(The special position given to the Catholic Church in the 1937 Irish Constitution was removed in 1972 and many of the above rules and laws of the Church and State are increasingly ignored in the Republic.

(Above) Jack Lynch is greeted on his visit to Stormont by Captain Terence O'Neill, Mrs O'Neill and members of the Cabinet.

Nevertheless, the steady decline of the Protestant population in the south, partly to be explained by heavy losses in the two world wars and the education of Protestant children at public schools in England who have tended not to return to Ireland, is considered by some in the north to be the result of the repression of Protestants. The northern suspicion of 'Rome Rule' remains strong.)

The Reverend Ian Paisley, the son of a Baptist preacher, (founder of the **Free Presbyterian Church** of Ulster in 1951, the Protestant Unionist Party in 1966 and the Democratic Unionist Party in 1971), strongly criticised any softening of relations towards the Republic or openness to Catholics. Even some colleagues in O'Neill's own cabinet considered his policies too liberal and there were attempts to remove him.

Tensions with the Republic

Improved relationships with the Republic did not last long. The 50th anniversaries, in 1966, of the **Easter Rising** and the **Battle of the Somme**, increased sectarian tensions in Northern Ireland. The increased pressure for reforms in Northern Ireland also created tension between the two governments. When Taoiseach Jack Lynch met with O'Neill in 1967,

Rev Ian Paisley leading a protest rally.

SOURCE A

A new generation of educated Catholics

There were stirrings of change among Catholics. The welfare state in general, and the Education Act in particular, made a rod for Stormont's back. A generation of Catholics, weaned on the welfare state, educated to a higher level than ever before, began to emerge from the late fifties. The number of Catholic students at Queen's University rose from 200 to 700 between 1955 and 1959 ....
Something approaching an independent-minded Catholic middle-class was beginning to emerge for the first time ....
*Relatively well-educated Catholics felt increasingly bitter at what they perceived as **discrimination**.*

J J Lee, *Ireland 1912–1985*, 1990, with the permission of Cambridge University Press

Paisley and his supporters protested with placards proclaiming 'O'Neill the **Lundy**' 'Keep Ulster Protestant' and 'O'Neill the Ally of Popery'. As the situation in Northern Ireland deteriorated, so did relations between Northern Ireland and the Republic.

Paisley's supporters protesting against the visit of Jack Lynch to Stormont.

SOURCE B

Nationalist and unionist views in Londonderry on the siting of the New University of Ulster at Coleraine

The issue of the location of Northern Ireland's second university is one of the greatest political scandals in the short history of Northern Ireland. Coming as it did after the creation of Craigavon to replace Derry as Northern Ireland's second city, after the closure of the rail link to Derry through the west, it was seen as the final act of a new unionist plantation of the east to the deliberate neglect of the west. The reaction to the decision was impassioned and spontaneous and transcended the sectarian and political divide in the City. For the first time since 1920, the people of Derry were united .... There are many who believe, with justification, that this was our last chance and that the university decision was the starting point of the difficulties and troubles that have beset .... the north of Ireland. The issue will become one of the greatest 'Ifs' in Irish history.

John Hume, 1972

John Hume.

Tensions with the new generation of educated Catholics

A younger generation of Catholics, who had benefited from free education for all under the welfare state, was not convinced that O'Neill meant to bring about change because of:

- the siting of the new city of Craigavon 30 miles from Belfast rather than in the economically depressed area west of the Bann;

- the naming of the new city after James Craig, Lord Craigavon, the first Prime Minister of Northern Ireland; and

- the siting of the new University of Ulster on a greenfield site in the small town of Coleraine rather than in the second largest city of Londonderry which was strongly Catholic. Both Protestants and Catholics from Derry joined together to petition the government about the decision.

SOURCE C

Allegations of discrimination against the west denied by government

The real problem was that there was usually much less local initiative there. In the richer, more populous and more go-ahead eastern parts there was always far more locally-generated drive, private and commercial as well as municipal.

John Oliver, Second Secretary in O'Neill's Ministry of Development 1964, speaking in 1971

ACTIVITIES

1 Why did some unionists object to O'Neill's policies?

2 Why did some Catholics object to O'Neill's policies?

3 Use Source A to identify reasons for the emergence, for the first time in Northern Ireland, of an independent-minded Catholic middle-class.

4 To what extent might Source C be considered to support Hume's view (Source B) that the government were deliberately neglecting the area west of the Bann?

Civil Rights

4.3

Ivan Cooper's first experience in politics was as a Young Unionist. He then became a member of the Northern Ireland Labour Party 1965–68 and was prominent in civil rights movement from earliest days. He was also MP for Mid-Derry at Stormont in 1969–1972.

> ### Focus
>
> **Why did the civil rights movement emerge when it did?**
>
> **What methods did they use and what were the results of the civil rights protests in 1968?**

During the 1960s, the civil rights campaign in the United States was reported throughout the world. Television pictures of black civil rights marchers inspired people in many countries. The Northern Ireland Civil Rights Association was formed in 1967.

The Civil Rights Association

The Northern Ireland Civil Rights Association was set up as a non-sectarian movement which aimed to bring about changes within Northern Ireland, as opposed to an end to partition. Its support was drawn from the Catholic middle-class, **nationalist** politicians, some Protestant liberals, trade unionists and members of the Northern Ireland Labour Party. It planned to adopt the same methods of non-violent protest that were being used by **Martin Luther King** and the **American civil rights movement**.

(Above) Police and civil rights protesters.

(Left) Martin Luther King leads a civil rights march in Alabama.

THE DEMANDS OF THE CIVIL RIGHTS ASSOCIATION:

- one man one vote (the right of everyone over 18 to vote and an end to extra votes for people owning businesses);

- an end to **gerrymandering** (which fixed constituency boundaries to create unionist control of Catholic areas);

- an end to discrimination in the allocation of government jobs;

- fair allocation of local council houses;

- the end of the Special Powers Act;

- the disbanding of the **B Specials**; and

- a formal complaints procedure against local authorities.

In August 1968, the first civil rights march took place from Coalisland to Dungannon. On 5 October, another civil rights march in Londonderry, which had been banned by the Unionist government, went ahead but ended in violence when the marchers were batoned by the police. The police action was seen on televisions around the world and provoked widespread indignation. Following further civil rights demonstrations, and pressure from Britain, O'Neill announced sweeping reforms of local government in Northern Ireland.

O'Neill's five point reforms

1 The appointment of an **Ombudsman** (to deal with complaints).

2 A points system for allocating council houses.

3 The replacement of Londonderry Corporation by a new Development Commission.

4 A review of the Special Powers Act.

5 The abolition of extra votes for businesses.

'One man one vote' in local government elections was not part of the package. Nevertheless, the civil rights movement agreed to call off all protests and marches to allow the reforms to begin.

> ## SOURCE B
>
> ### The impact of British intervention on civil rights
>
> *In just 48 days since 5 October 1968 the Catholic minority had won more political concessions than it had over the previous 47 years.*
>
> **J Bardon, A History of Ulster, 1992, with the permission of The Blackstaff Press Ltd**

> ## SOURCE A
>
> ### Influences upon the civil rights movement
>
> *The whole civil rights scene had been infected by the television images in 1968 of direct action, whether in France, Germany or America.*
>
> **B White, John Hume, Statesman of the Troubles, 1984**

ACTIVITIES

1 What evidence is there to suggest that the civil rights movement was inspired by the black movement for civil rights led by Martin Luther King in America?

2 After such a long period of leaving unionists to govern Northern Ireland without interference, why do you think the British government put pressure on O'Neill to respond to the demands of the civil rights movement?

3 Which of the civil rights demands were granted in O'Neill's Five Point Plan and which were withheld?

The Fall of O'Neill

> ## Focus
>
> **Why did O'Neill have only limited success in his attempt 'to build bridges' within the community?**

Despite O'Neill's five point plan the civil rights campaign continued. A new socialist/nationalist group called The People's Democracy (PD), emerged in Belfast led mainly by university students like Bernadette Devlin, later elected to Westminster as the youngest ever MP. The Civil Rights Association called for a temporary end to protests but the People's Democracy group ignored this plea and organised a march from Belfast to Londonderry in January 1969.

The People's Democracy march

The march sparked off anger as it passed through Protestant areas and was ambushed by **loyalists** at Burntollet Bridge near Londonderry. The marchers were stoned and beaten with sticks and cudgels. Some of the attackers were believed to be off-duty policemen and B Specials. The police escort appeared to do little to stop them. O'Neill braved the anger of his own party by announcing a commission of inquiry into the disturbances. Brian Faulkner, his Deputy Prime Minister, resigned in protest arguing that an inquiry, whatever its findings, could only make the situation worse. Despite O'Neill's willingness to set up an inquiry, Catholics lost further confidence in the government and the RUC. Civil rights marches began again.

Bernadette Devlin.

SOURCE   A

Smash Stormont

SMASH

UNIONIST JUNTA

STORMONT

People's Democracy poster

Police clash with People's Democracy marchers in Lurgan.

Civil rights demonstrators in Dungannon prepare to retaliate.

SOURCE B

An historian's view of the symbolism of the PD march

*People's Democracy ....
insisted on marching through
traditionally Protestant
territory, en route from Belfast
to Derry. Some of the
participants imagined they
were engaged on an Ulster
version of the Selma to
Montgomery March (a re-
enactment of a famous black
march through the white
dominated southern states
of America).*

**J J Lee, *Ireland 1912–85*, 1990,
with the permission of
Cambridge University Press**

O'Neill seeks electoral support for his policies

O'Neill's position was now so shaken that he had little hope of survival unless he could mobilise massive public support. He called a general election in February 1969. Two hundred and thirty thousand people voted for pro-O'Neill candidates, as opposed to the 120,000 who voted against them, but, despite the fact that a greater number of people voted pro-O'Neill, his candidates did not succeed in winning a large enough majority of seats to put his government in a position of strength. The split in unionist ranks during the election, and the narrowness of his personal victory over Ian Paisley in his own Bannside constituency, further weakened O'Neill's position. When he decided he would grant 'one man one vote' at the next local government elections, his cousin, the Minister of Agriculture, James Chichester-Clark, resigned. O'Neill himself resigned shortly afterwards, realising that he was unlikely to be able to carry the support of his colleagues much longer.

SOURCE C

Basic fear of Protestants

The basic fear of Protestants in Northern Ireland is that they will be outbred by Roman Catholics. It is as simple as that. It is frightfully hard to explain to a Protestant that if you give a Roman Catholic a good house they will live like Protestants .... They will refuse to have 18 children. But if the Roman Catholic is jobless and lives in a ghastly hovel, he will rear 18 children on national assistance. It is impossible to explain this to a militant Protestant, because he is so keen to deny civil rights to his Roman Catholic neighbours. He cannot understand, in fact, that if you treat Roman Catholics with due consideration and kindness they will live like Protestants, in spite of the authoritative nature of their church.

O'Neill's views from a speech shortly after resigning

SOURCE D

An historian's verdict of O'Neill

O'Neill explained his dilemma in his autobiography: 'As the Party would never stand for change, I was really reduced to trying to improve relations between north and south; and in the north itself between the two sections of the community. In this respect I think I can truthfully say that I succeeded'.

There was ample evidence that he had done much to ease tensions between the majority and the minority, despite the criticism of loyalist conservatives. O'Neill, however, had raised Catholic expectations but found himself unable to deliver more than gestures of friendship: thoroughgoing reform did not follow and the result was acute frustration.

J Bardon, *A History of Ulster*, 1992, with the permission of The Blackstaff Press Ltd

SOURCE E

One of the reasons why O'Neill failed, an historian's view

The committee announced a month's moratorium on demonstrations in response to O'Neill's initiative. Had a breathing space developed it is just conceivable, if still highly unlikely, that a modicum of civilised change might have proved possible. O'Neill needed time to consolidate the apparently emerging centre.

J J Lee, *Ireland 1912–85*, 1990, with the permission of Cambridge University Press

ACTIVITIES

1 Why did the civil rights movement appear to become more militant in 1969 and where did the militant influences come from?

2 Using Sources A and B (pages 103-104), identify the motives of the People's Democracy movement in continuing to protest.

3 Source C, the speech which O'Neill made shortly after resigning, enraged both Protestants and Catholics. Why do you think this was so?

4 What does Source D suggest about O'Neill's chances of settling the situation in Northern Ireland in December 1968 and why did the 'breathing space' fail to develop?

5 What does Source E suggest about O'Neill's chances of success?

Westminster Intervenes

Focus

Why did the Republic threaten to intervene in Northern Ireland in 1969 and how real was the threat?

Why did Westminster decide to intervene in Northern Ireland in 1969 and what were the results?

During July and August 1969 violence in Northern Ireland worsened and the new Prime Minister, James Chichester-Clark, mobilised the B Specials to support the RUC. This provoked further Catholic resentment.

The sectarian summer of 1969

Fierce fighting erupted in Londonderry on 12 August 1969 after the **Apprentice Boys** parade through the city. Catholic rioters and the RUC fought each other for three days using tear gas, petrol bombs and rubber bullets. This battle for control of the Catholic **Bogside** area was captured on television and did much to damage the image of the RUC. At the same time, serious **sectarian** violence erupted in Belfast. Rows of houses were burned to the ground and 3,500, mostly Catholic, families were driven from their homes. Seven people were killed and about 100 wounded as gunfire replaced stones and petrol bombs. The Republic's Prime Minister, Jack Lynch, threatened to intervene and Irish army units were moved to the border. Field hospitals were opened to deal with refugees from the north.

SOURCE A

The existence of Northern Ireland under threat

The monster of sectarian violence is well out of its cage. The issue now is no longer civil rights, or even houses and jobs. The issue now is whether the state should exist.

The Sunday Times, August 1969

The Battle of the Bogside, August 1969.

A group of men carry the remains of their belongings past burning buildings during disturbances in Belfast.

British troops sent in

The Labour Prime Minister, Harold Wilson, decided that the situation was out of control. On 15 August he ordered British troops into Belfast and Londonderry to relieve the exhausted RUC. The troops were welcomed by Catholics as protectors. For the first time since the **Anglo-Irish Treaty of 1921**, the British government was again involved directly in Irish affairs. The Downing Street Declaration of 19 August 1969 forced the Stormont government to introduce further reforms:

- the reorganisation of the RUC;

- the creation of a new Ministry of Community Relations;

- an independent Community Relations Commission;

- the establishment of a Commission of Complaints;

- reform of the local government **franchise** (one man one vote and new election boundaries to end gerrymandering);

- measures to prevent discrimination in the allocation of public jobs;

SOURCE B

The south threatens to intervene

It is evident that the Stormont government is no longer in control .... the Irish government can no longer stand by and see innocent people injured and perhaps worse.

Jack Lynch, Irish Prime Minister, August 1969

British troops arriving at the naval dockyard in Londonderry.

An army 'snatch squad' in action.

SOURCE C

The threat of southern intervention: an historian's view

Despite Lynch's mutterings, the south could not intervene even if it wanted to. Lynch's gesture had presumably been primarily to encourage British intervention. The south, having taken no serious steps to be in a position to defend itself since independence, was in even less of a position to defend Belfast Catholics.

J J Lee, *Ireland 1912–85*, 1990, with the permission of Cambridge University Press

- a **'points' system** to ensure fair allocation of local authority housing; and

- an enquiry into security (the Hunt Report) which later recommended: the abolition of the B Specials, to be replaced by a new Ulster Defence Regiment under the control of the British Army.

It was hoped that once British standards of justice were seen to be implemented, life in Northern Ireland would return to normal. The civil rights leaders, surprised to see their programme officially adopted, had no further specific plans for political activity.

ACTIVITIES

1 In Source A (page 106), the writer says the issue now is no longer civil rights …. the issue now is whether the state should exist. Explain what he meant.

2 Describe the reactions to the violence of 1969 by:
   (a) the Unionist government;
   (b) the Irish government; and
   (c) the British government

   and give possible explanations for each reaction.

3 Suggest as many reasons as you can to explain why violence erupted in Northern Ireland in 1969.

The Revival of the IRA
and Perspectives on Civil Rights

4.6

Focus

Why did the IRA revive in 1969?

Why did some Protestants view the civil rights campaign as a republican plot to destroy the Northern Ireland state?

During the 1950s and 1960s Catholics in Northern Ireland shared in the benefits of the welfare state. As a result, nationalist interest in the struggle for a united Ireland declined. The **Irish Republican Army (IRA)** abandoned a campaign which they had mounted in Northern Ireland between 1956 and 1962 due to lack of interest and support from the Catholic population in the north. The governments of Northern Ireland and the Republic both used internment without trial to lock up IRA activists. The IRA decided to turn towards socialism. The weakness and inability of the IRA to protect the Catholic population during the sectarian attacks of August 1969 prompted people to claim that the letters IRA stood for 'I ran away'. Brian Faulkner later admitted that the IRA was in no position to take effective action in 1969.

The rise of extremists

As a reaction to the sectarian attacks of 1969, a new militant IRA began to organise and quickly built up support, particularly in Belfast. In 1970 this new, more militant grouping split from the older **'Official' IRA**, whom they

A row of houses ablaze during disturbances in Belfast.

SOURCE A

The commanding officer of a British battalion that served in the Falls in 1972–73

The burning of Bombay Street was the oft repeated and most regarded underlying justification for the IRA's claim to be needed as the only defence force that the Catholics of Belfast could rely on in dire emergency to protect their lives and homes. The bulk of the Catholic population accepted this claim, and justification of the IRA, and although many of them thoroughly dislike the bombing and murdering by the IRA, they were not prepared to co-operate with the forces of the Crown to destroy the IRA, just in case another Bombay Street situation might arise.

R Evelegh, Peace-keeping in a Democratic Society: The Lessons of Northern Ireland, 1978, with the permission of C Hurst & Company Ltd

IRA recruitment poster.

SUPPORT YOUR LOCAL UNIT

UVF poster.

accused of having gone soft on the struggle for a united Ireland. They formed the '**Provisional**' **IRA** and began a ruthless and savage campaign of violence which aimed to destroy the Northern Ireland state and to force the British to withdraw completely from Ireland.

Between 1970 and 1971 the Provisional IRA attacked both soldiers and the police and bombed businesses and shops. Civilian riots and clashes with army and police also claimed lives. The death toll rose sharply from 13 deaths in 1969 to 25 in 1970 to 174 in 1971. The IRA campaign convinced many Protestants that Catholics would never be satisfied until they achieved a united Ireland. Protestant **paramilitary** groups, such as the Ulster Volunteer Force (UVF), began using IRA style tactics to defend Ulster and the union from the IRA. Loyalist paramilitaries claimed responsibility for an explosion in McGurk's Bar in December 1971 which killed 15 people.

Protestant views of the civil rights campaign

- Many middle-class Protestants were genuinely shocked at the revelations of discrimination in the late 1960s and agreed with O'Neill's steps towards reforms.

- Continued protests made some Protestants feel that the civil rights movement was pushing too hard too fast and that Catholics would never be satisfied.

- Working-class Protestants living in poor housing conditions resented the attention given to civil rights demands and felt 'civil rights' meant 'Catholic rights'.

- Other Protestants believed that the old enemy, the IRA, was controlling the civil rights movement as a first step towards a united Ireland.

SOURCE B

A Shankill housewife's view

It was all the Catholics this, the Catholics that, living in poverty and us lording it over them. People looked around and said 'What, are they talking about us? With the damp running down the walls and the houses not fit to live in'.

S Nelson, *Ulster's Uncertain Defenders*, 1984, with the permission of The Appletree Press Ltd

SOURCE C

Protestants mistook the motives behind civil rights: an historian's view

Instead of ignoring the parliament and government of Northern Ireland, Catholics started to demand changes .... Almost inevitably, the majority of Northern Ireland Protestants regarded the resultant civil rights movement as a front for an IRA assault on the border .... This mistake in identity did indeed give opponents of the border their opportunity. A movement for reform within the existing constitution was turned into an attack upon the very existence of Northern Ireland. Once again the British government was faced with the problem of reconciling the fears of Ulster unionists with the aspirations of Irish nationalists.

P Buckland, *Irish Unionism: Two*, 1973, with the permission of Gill and Macmillan Ltd (adapted)

Protestant women voice their disgust at the Civil Rights' campaign.

ACTIVITIES

1 What does Source A (page 109) suggest was the reason for the revival of the IRA and the support it received from the Catholic community?

2 How may the Shankhill housewife's views (Source B) about civil rights have been affected by her way of life?

3 The author of Source C suggests that almost inevitably, the majority of Northern Ireland Protestants regarded the resultant civil rights movement as a front for an IRA assault on the border. Why do you think a lot of Protestants formed this view about the civil rights movement?

4 Is it fair to say that **all** Protestants were opposed to civil rights demands? Explain your answer.

5 Using the information in this section, explain how each of these people may have reacted to the civil rights movement:
   (a) a British minister;
   (b) a supporter of O'Neill;
   (c) a supporter of the Rev Ian Paisley.

6 In your view, to what extent is the view that the civil rights movement was a republican plot justified or unjustified? Give reasons for your answer.

The Situation Deteriorates

4.7

Focus

Why did unrest in Northern Ireland get worse, rather than better, after British troops arrived in August 1969?

The political implications of putting British troops onto the streets of Northern Ireland under the control of the government at Stormont had not been thought through. The troops could gain a breathing space for the politicians but the army could not impose a solution, because there was no political solution to impose.

Arms searches

The army was placed under the control of the Unionist government and found itself in a complex situation. It had been sent into Northern Ireland to prevent civil war but its presence provided the IRA, determined to destroy the state, with an ideal target. If the army did nothing but wait, the IRA might gradually acquire the resources to mount an aggressive campaign against it. If the army moved against the IRA it could be interpreted that they were on the side of unionists and against Catholics. In effect, the army became *piggy in the middle* (a phrase used by D Hamill in the title of his book, *Pig in the Middle: The Army in Northern Ireland*, 1985).

The decision was taken to search Catholic areas for arms. The arms searches were an attempt to crush the IRA before they became a serious threat, but they served only to increase IRA recruitment. In 1970, a 34 hour curfew was imposed on the Catholic Falls Road to allow arms searches to take place. In 1971, 17,262 house searches were carried out. Of the 1,183 houses searched between November 1971 and January 1972, arms were found in only 47.

SOURCE A

Arms searches 'a political disaster'

The army made more enemies by using CS gas against the rioters, thus achieving the Provo objective .... The 34 hour curfew imposed on the Falls in July 1970 to facilitate arms searches was .... in political terms, a disaster.

D Hamill, *Pig in the Middle: The Army in Northern Ireland*, 1985, with the permission of Methuen London Ltd (adapted)

SOURCE B

Arms searches alienate the population

Without inside information as to the exact whereabouts of terrorist weapons and documents, the security forces have little option but to search on the vaguest suspicions – nothing is more certain to alienate the population.

R Evelegh, *Peacekeeping in a Democratic Society: The Lessons of Northern Ireland*, 1978, with the permission of C Hurst & Company Ltd

The army carries out a search.

SOURCE

Initial welcome of army quickly disappeared

That the Provisionals achieved widespread support among Belfast Catholics .... was due more to the British army than to themselves. For the army made rapid progress in translating the initial Catholic welcome firstly into suspicion and then into hate.

J J Lee, *Ireland 1912–85*, 1990, with the permission of Cambridge University Press

New political groupings

New political groupings began to emerge. The break up of the Unionist Party became more pronounced when Ian Paisley won the Bannside by-election on 17 April 1970. Four days later, some liberal unionists who were dedicated to reform and reconciliation, formed the nucleus of the Alliance Party which aimed to bridge the growing divide between Catholic and Protestant. Shortly afterwards, in August 1970, nationalist, socialist, liberal and labour politicians came together to form the Social Democratic and Labour Party (SDLP) which, although it did have a few Protestant members, immediately became the principal voice of the Catholic minority.

(Below far left) Alliance poster.

(Below middle) Gerry Fitt, leader of the SDLP.

(Below) SDLP election poster.

Internment

In August 1971 the Unionist government used the Special Powers Act to introduce '**internment**', the power to arrest, interrogate and detain without trial anyone suspected of being involved in the IRA. The army relied on information which the RUC had on the old IRA. As a result, of the 2,357 people arrested during the first six months, 1,600 were released after interrogation. Few senior members of the Provisional IRA were detained. The Northern Ireland Prime Minister, Brian Faulkner, actually refused to sign detention orders for 97 of the first 337 suspects and later admitted that *many of the most wanted escaped the net.*

Internment not only failed to stop the violence, but increased support and sympathy for the IRA. Casualties soared in the months immediately after internment. Thirty people had been killed before 9 August 1971, the date of the introduction of internment. By the end of 1971, 143 had been killed. Internment became a new focus for civil rights protests as well as a nationalist **rent and rates strike**, called by the SDLP.

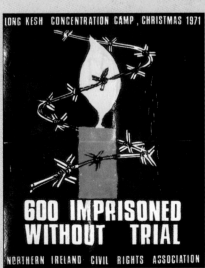

Civil Rights anti-internment poster.

Bloody Sunday

In January 1972, a huge civil rights march took place in Londonderry to protest against internment. Rioting broke out as the rally broke up. Claiming that they were fired on, British army paratroopers opened fire on the marchers and 13 civilians were killed. The subsequent Widgery inquiry, set up by the British government, failed to establish that any of the victims were armed.

This incident, known as Bloody Sunday, was followed by rioting in nationalist areas and an increase in the IRA's bombing campaign.

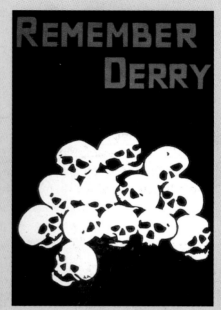

(Above) Peoples' Democracy poster commemorating 'Bloody Sunday'.

(Top left) Demonstrators scurry through the streets as soldiers use CS gas.

(Bottom left) Mourners at St Mary's church paying their respects to the victims of 'Bloody Sunday'.

ACTIVITIES

1   In what way did arms searches and internment affect the attitudes of Catholics in Northern Ireland towards the Unionist government and the army?

2   Identify as many reasons as you can to explain why the army's role in Northern Ireland became increasingly difficult.

The Fall of Stormont

Focus

What was the reaction of different sections of the population in Northern Ireland to the imposition of direct rule in 1972?

Fearing that law and order was about to break down completely, Brian Faulkner, the Northern Ireland Prime Minister, demanded authority to rearm the RUC and re-establish the B Specials. Instead, the British **Conservative** Prime Minister, Edward Heath, insisted on complete British control of security, including the RUC, as well as full responsibility for law and order, justice and the appointment of judges. When Faulkner and his Cabinet refused, Edward Heath took the decision in March 1972 to suspend the Stormont parliament and to introduce direct rule of Northern Ireland from Westminster.

Direct rule

Direct rule from London was intended as a temporary measure until a new system of government for Northern Ireland could be agreed. For the time being, decisions and laws governing Northern Ireland were to be made in Westminster. A Secretary of State and a small team of junior ministers were appointed to take control of departments, such as education, health and social services. Unionists were assured that any change in the status of Northern Ireland would only be by *the consent of the majority of the people of Northern Ireland* while nationalists were promised the same rights as other British citizens.

Reactions to the introduction of direct rule

There was a wide range of reactions to the British government's decision to introduce direct rule.

- Many in the unionist community felt betrayed by the British government and some began to support more extreme parties. Support for Protestant paramilitary organisations increased and the paramilitary Ulster Defence Association (UDA) was formed. There was an increased spate of sectarian murders, particularly in Belfast.

- Many nationalists were pleased, as it brought an end to unionist control and gave hope for a better future but the Civil Rights Association and the People's Democracy movement continued their campaign for reform.

- The Dublin government welcomed direct rule and called for an IRA cease-fire.

- The IRA viewed direct rule as Britain *seeking to claim a country to which it had no legal right*. It escalated its campaign of violence.

22 bombs – Belfast – Bloody Friday

(Above) Loyalists demonstrate against the suspension of Stormont.

SOURCE

IRA lost an opportunity for peace, an historian's view

It is arguable that the (Provos) lost their best opportunity of acquiring a political profile at that time by failing to announce a ceasefire immediately on the introduction of direct rule, and publicising realistic conditions for a cessation of hostilities. That they did not do so presumably indicates how close to forcing British withdrawal they thought themselves to be. And they may, of course, have been racked by internal dissension on the matter. The safest way to avoid dissension was to insist on total victory .... In June 1972 (in talks after the ceasefire) the IRA pitched its demands unrealistically high, and the more militaristic elements quickly resumed hostilities.

The UDA on the march.

Temporary truce

Neither internment nor direct rule had any significant effect on the violence. Four hundred and sixty-seven people were killed in Northern Ireland in 1972, the highest death toll for any of the 25 years of the troubles. The escalation of IRA violence was so severe that the new Secretary of State, William Whitelaw, consented to talks in London with the IRA. A temporary IRA **ceasefire** was called but the terms of the IRA deal, a complete withdrawal of British troops and an **amnesty** for all political prisoners, were unacceptable. The IRA signalled the end of the ceasefire by exploding 26 car bombs in Belfast on Bloody Friday, 21 July 1972. The toll of that one day was 11 dead and 130 injured.

SOURCE B

Opportunity for peace lost after the ceasefire: an historian's view

By breaking their ceasefire the Provisionals lost their best opportunity in two decades to negotiate terms for the people they claimed to protect. Their ruthless bombing campaign gave the SDLP the opportunity to climb down from its unproductive abstentionist position.

J Bardon, *A History of Ulster*, 1992, with the permission of The Blackstaff Press Ltd

ACTIVITIES

1 Why did Edward Heath take the decision to suspend Stormont?

2 Explain the reasons for some of the different reactions to the fall of Stormont and the imposition of direct rule from Westminster.

3 To what extent do Sources A and B agree about the opportunities for peace in 1972?

What reasons does Source A suggest to explain why the Provisional IRA did not use the opportunity?

Attempts at a Solution

4.9

Focus

What form of government was agreed for Northern Ireland in 1973–74?

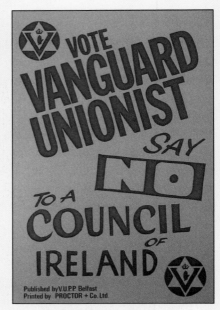

Vanguard Unionist poster.

Before Britain could allow local politicians to govern Northern Ireland again, Britain insisted that agreement would have to be reached between unionists and nationalists on how Northern Ireland should be governed. For the first time, the British government acknowledged an 'Irish dimension' and agreed that Dublin should be consulted about, and have some input into, how Northern Ireland should be governed in the future.

A power-sharing assembly

In March 1973, plans for an Assembly in which unionists and nationalists would share power, were announced by the British government. Brian Faulkner, the leader of the Ulster Unionist Party, agreed to take part in the Assembly although he promised his supporters he would never share power with *any party whose primary objective is to break the union with Britain.* Other unionists totally opposed **power-sharing** and left the Unionist Party to form the more extreme Vanguard Unionist Progressive Party. An election was held for an assembly of all parties in June 1973. Most seats were won by the parties which supported power-sharing.

PARTY	POWER-SHARING	SEATS	% OF VOTES
Faulkner Unionists	YES	24	29.3
Other Unionists	NO	26	32.6
SDLP	YES	19	22.1
Alliance	YES	8	9.2
Northern Ireland Labour Party	YES	1	2.6

Ulster Unionist poster.

A power-sharing executive

Only the parties supporting power-sharing were invited to form the power-sharing Executive which was to govern Northern Ireland. The membership of the Executive was eventually agreed in November 1973, but a number of problems remained.

- Politicians opposed to power-sharing were not consulted about the new system.

- Nationalists were concerned that unionists had been given too many seats in the Executive so that, if they voted together, their built-in majority would defeat any opposition.

- The nature of the Republic of Ireland's role in Northern Ireland affairs had yet to be defined.

An Irish dimension: the Sunningdale Agreement

Before the power-sharing Executive could take office, a conference was held at Sunningdale in Berkshire to discuss Northern Ireland's future relations with the Republic. Delegations from Britain and both parts of Ireland took part in the conference, including Edward Heath, the British Prime Minister, the Republic's Taoiseach, Liam Cosgrave, and the leaders of the power-sharing parties in Northern Ireland's Assembly. Unionists opposed to power-sharing were not invited to take part in the talks.

All the delegates at Sunningdale welcomed a power-sharing executive for Northern Ireland but it proved much more difficult to get an agreement on an 'Irish dimension'. After a great deal of discussion, it was decided to set up a Council of Ireland. The Council would have seven members from each part of Ireland and would work to improve relations on the island.

Handshakes after the signing of the Sunningdale Agreement, December 1973.

Brian Faulkner believed he could convince unionists they had nothing to fear from power-sharing and the Council of Ireland. On 9 December, he signed the Sunningdale Agreement. The British government was pleased at what had been achieved although the role of a Council of Ireland remained unclear.

- Brian Faulkner saw the Council as an advisory body to help improve economic relations in Ireland.

- John Hume, an SDLP member of the Executive, saw it as a way to gradually increase political links with the Republic.

- British politicians saw it as a way to encourage nationalists to become more involved in the political life of Northern Ireland.

- The southern delegates thought the Council would improve relations between Northern Ireland and the Republic which might lay the foundations for the eventual reunification of Ireland.

ACTIVITIES

1 What percentage of voters in Northern Ireland supported power-sharing and what percentage of these were unionist?

2 Why was the Sunningdale Conference held and what was agreed at it?

3 What aspects of the Sunningdale Agreement were likely to give rise to unionist opposition?

Power-sharing

Focus

What problems did the power-sharing Executive face in 1974?

After the successful negotiations at Sunningdale the British government announced that the power-sharing Executive would become responsible for governing Northern Ireland from 1 January 1974. But even before the Executive took office, in January 1974, there were doubts about its chances of success.

Problems facing the Executive

- Some members of the Executive found it difficult to work with politicians from other parties.

- Supporters of power-sharing feared their interests would be sacrificed to make the power-sharing administration work.

- The Executive was heavily criticised by unionists opposed to the Sunningdale Agreement.

- Unionist parties opposed to the Sunningdale Agreement joined forces to disrupt business in the Assembly.

- Britain was still responsible for Northern Ireland's security policy, but the Executive was blamed for not stopping the high level of violence.

- The Irish government did not officially recognise Northern Ireland or introduce extradition (laws to allow people suspected of committing violent crime in Northern Ireland to be returned there to stand trial for the offences).

- There were also serious differences of opinion about the role of a Council of Ireland.

SOURCE B

Dublin is just a Sunningdale away

United Ulster Unionist Coalition election poster.

(Below) William Whitelaw.

SOURCE A

The Northern Ireland Executive's chances of success

The Observer, 25 November 1973.

The 1974 election

Just two months after the Executive took office, the British government called a general election. Eleven of the 12 Northern Ireland seats at Westminster were won by parties opposed to the Sunningdale Agreement. Unionists opposed to power-sharing said the election results proved the Executive did not represent the views of the people. The deputy leader of the Executive, Gerry Fitt, argued that the election had come too soon and people did not yet understand what Sunningdale was about. Anti-Sunningdale unionists demanded new assembly elections but their request was ignored.

The return of a Labour government in Britain, and a fresh IRA bombing campaign in March and April, increased unionist fears about the Sunningdale Agreement because the Labour Party was considered much less supportive of the union than the Conservatives. Nevertheless, the result of an opinion poll taken in early April 1974, was still reasonably encouraging about power-sharing but highlighted strong unionist opposition to an Irish dimension.

SOURCE D

Nationalist view of Sunningdale

The general approach of the SDLP to the (Sunningdale) talks was to get all Ireland institutions established .... which could lead ultimately to an agreed single state for Ireland.

Paddy Devlin, SDLP delegate at Sunningdale, speaking in 1975

SOURCE C

Results of the opinion poll on the Sunningdale Agreement taken between 31 March and 7 April 1974

(i) Do you approve or disapprove of power within the Executive being shared?

	Protestant %	Catholic %
Approve strongly	28	78
Just approve	38	16
Don't know	13	5
Just disapprove	9	1
Disapprove strongly	13	1

(ii) Do you think that the Sunningdale proposal for a Council of Ireland is a good or bad idea?

	Protestant %	Catholic %
Good idea	26	72
Bad idea	52	4
Have not heard of proposals	3	6
Don't know	19	18

ACTIVITIES

1 How safe did the cartoonist in Source A (page 121) consider the new Northern Ireland power-sharing executive to be?
This cartoon was drawn before the Sunningdale Agreement was signed. If it had been drawn afterwards what other 'clouds' might the cartoonist have added?

 Examine Source C. What percentage of opinion on both sides of the community in 1974 favoured:
(a) power-sharing?
(b) a Council of Ireland?

3 In what ways do Sources B and D (pages 121-122) help to explain unionist anxiety about the role of a Council of Ireland?

The Ulster Workers' Strike

> ## *Focus*
>
> **Why did Protestant workers strike in 1974?**
>
> **What effect did the strike have upon the attempt at power-sharing in Northern Ireland?**

After the demands of anti-power-sharing unionists for new assembly elections were ignored, some unionists felt nothing would be achieved by using normal political methods. They began to look for other ways to get rid of the Executive and the Sunningdale Agreement. In late 1973, a group of Protestant trade unionists formed the Ulster Workers' Council to organise action against government plans considered 'unacceptable' to unionists. The Council was joined in 1974 by loyalist paramilitaries and anti-power-sharing politicians.

Protest against 'an Irish dimension'

When demands for new Assembly elections were ignored, the UWC warned it would call a strike if the power-sharing Executive continued to support the Sunningdale Agreement. On 14 May 1974, the new Northern Ireland Assembly voted in favour of continuing with the Sunningdale Agreement. (Parties in favour of power-sharing still held the majority in the Assembly.) After hearing the decision, the Ulster Worker's Council called for a general strike.

No-one was sure if the strike-call was serious so the strike was slow to start. After a few days, a newly formed UWC Strike Co-ordinating Committee started to organise the stoppage. It was only at the end of the first week, however, that the government realised how serious the situation had become. Road blocks had been erected and most industries had been forced to close because electricity supplies and the distribution of petrol were controlled by the strikers. As the strike continued, it won the

(Above) Queuing for petrol.

(Below) Queuing for dole.

support of most unionists. Efforts were made to persuade people to go back to work but a 'back-to-work' march, organised by the trade unions, ended in failure.

The British government refused to negotiate with the strikers. The Prime Minister Harold Wilson, in a television broadcast on the 25 May, described the strikers as *people who spend their lives sponging on Westminster and British democracy.* Many people in Northern Ireland were outraged by Wilson's comments. It made the strikers more determined to continue. The Army warned that it would be difficult to defeat the strikers and advised the British government against using soldiers to try to break the strike. As the situation deteriorated, the SDLP agreed reluctantly to delay the introduction of the Council of Ireland. The UWC said this was too little too late.

When the government ordered the Army to take control of petrol stations and oil depots on 27 May, the UWC called for a total shut-down. Fearing for the health and safety of the community, Faulkner, the Chief Executive of the power-sharing Executive, asked the Secretary of State, Merlyn Rees, to negotiate with the strikers. Rees refused. Faulkner felt he had no choice but to resign from his post of Chief Executive and the other unionist members of the power-sharing Executive resigned with him. Their resignations brought the power-sharing Executive to an end. The UWC strike was called off on 29 May and Northern Ireland was returned to government by direct rule.

SOURCE A

British government attitude towards the strikers

The people on this side of the water – British parents – have seen our sons spat upon and murdered. British taxpayers have seen the taxes they have poured out, going to Northern Ireland. They see property destroyed by evil violence and are asked to pick up the bill for rebuilding it. Yet people who benefit from this now viciously defy Westminster, people who spend their lives sponging on Westminster and British democracy. Who do these people think they are?

Harold Wilson, British Prime Minister, 25 May 1974

(Above) The 'back-to-work' march entering the Harbour Estate Belfast, during the strike.

(Right) Loyalists celebrate the fall of the Executive.

SOURCE B

Effect of Wilson's speech

Any hope he (Wilson) had of wrecking the strike went with that speech.

Glen Barr, UWC Strike Committee chairman, 1975

SOURCE C

Southern view

The Executive has been wrecked by deliberate misrepresentation of its purpose on the one hand and by the continuance of (IRA) violence on the other.

Taoiseach Liam Cosgrave in a speech in the Dáil, 28 May 1974

SOURCE D

Southern view

The Executive was shattered by what they saw as their betrayal by the British government that seemed to them .... to be frightened of its own Army.

Garret FitzGerald, a member of the Irish government in 1974, from his memoirs, *All in a Life*, 1991, with the permission of Gill and Macmillan Ltd

SOURCE E

British view

The power-sharing Executive was brought down by the UWC, the United Ulster Unionist Council and the majority community .... There was a feeling of tit-for-tat: the republicans had toppled Stormont, the loyalists had now brought down the Executive.

Merlyn Rees, the Secretary of State for Northern Ireland in 1974, from his memoirs, *Northern Ireland: A Personal Perspective*, 1985, with the permission of Methuen London Ltd

Brian Faulkner announcing the resignation of the Unionist ministers from the Executive on 28 May 1974.

Violence continues

IRA and sectarian violence continued. Two hundred and fifty people were killed in 1973 and 216 in 1974. In October and November 1974, the IRA attempted to put further pressure on Britain to withdraw by exploding bombs in Guildford and Birmingham, killing 24 people and injuring 247.

SOURCE F

Unionist view

The power-sharing Executive .... did not succeed .... because we presented it inadequately, because the IRA was able to step up its terrorist campaign, because neither the British nor the Irish governments was prepared to take difficult decisions and give us (the Executive) consistent backing when it was most needed.

Brian Faulkner, from *Memoirs of a Statesman*, 1978, with the permission of Weidenfeld and Nicolson Publishers

ACTIVITIES

1   Explain why the Ulster Workers Council called a strike on 14 May 1974.

2   Describe the tactics used by the UWC Strike Co-ordinating Committee to bring about the strike.

3   Was the UWC strike successful? Explain your answer.

4   Using all the sources, make a list of reasons to explain the fall of the Executive.

5   Explain how the background and work of the authors of Sources C, D, E and F (pages 125-126) may have influenced their views on the reasons for the fall of the Executive.

'The Bullet and the Ballot Box'

> ## Focus
>
> **How and why did the IRA decide to seek political support from 1980?**
>
> **What effect did Sinn Féin's electoral success have upon the situation in Northern Ireland?**

The British government believed it had a responsibility to restore a form of agreed government to Northern Ireland. Between 1974 and 1984, various Secretaries of State, Merlyn Rees, Roy Mason, Humphrey Atkins and James Prior, all made attempts to get an internal political settlement but failed for one reason or another. A powerful and emotional response by women to the tragic deaths of three children from the Maguire family, who were crushed against a fence by a wounded gunman in a getaway car, led to the setting up of the Peace People in 1976. In such a deeply divided society, however, it proved difficult to sustain widespread support. A second IRA ceasefire collapsed in 1975, and the IRA continued with its campaign. The death toll remained high, 247 in 1975 rising to nearly 300 in 1976, although increased intelligence and undercover work began to take its toll on the IRA. They reorganised into smaller secret cells. Some in the political wing wanted to become more active in politics.

The H blocks (the Maze Prison).

Special category status for political prisoners

In the early 1970s people convicted of crimes related to the political violence were given special category status, which meant they were not treated as 'criminals' but as 'political prisoners of war'. They were allowed to wear their own clothes and did not have to do prison work. After 1976, the British government decided to remove special category status and treat all prisoners as criminals, regardless of their offences.

IRA prisoners in the H Blocks (the Maze Prison) and the women's prison at Armagh refused to co-operate with the changes in prison rules. They chose to wear blankets instead of prison uniforms. The protest became known as the '**blanket protest**' and, later, the '**dirty protest**' when prisoners refused to wash or slop out their toilet buckets. The British government refused to restore political status. Prisoners' relatives and supporters began a campaign to highlight their protests but few people were interested.

1981 hunger strike

Hunger strikes had been used as a strategy by republicans in the 1920s, 1940s, 1972 and 1974 to bring pressure to bear on the British government. In 1980, a number of republican prisoners decided to go on hunger strike to regain '**political status**'. The campaign gained wide support in nationalist areas and huge protest marches and rallies were held. The first

Smash H blocks poster.

hunger strike was called off in December 1980 because the strikers believed they had gained some of their demands. This was not the case. Three months later, a second hunger strike began, led by Bobby Sands, the IRA commander in the **H Block compounds** at the Maze Prison.

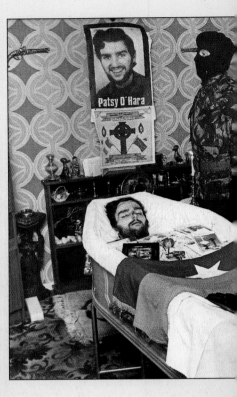

(Left) Marching in support of the prisoners' demands.

The hunger strikers gained support from many Catholics in Northern Ireland and elsewhere who, although not supporters of the IRA, had sympathy for their demands. With the intention of putting more pressure on the British government, Bobby Sands stood as a candidate in the 1981 Fermanagh/South Tyrone election and was elected as a Westminster MP. The support for Sands shocked many Protestants who viewed the hunger strikers as gunmen and murderers. Despite the pressure from other governments and the media, Margaret Thatcher refused to make concessions. Sands and nine other hunger strikers died before the campaign was called off, under pressure from relatives. Shortly afterwards, some of the hunger strikers demands were granted.

Results of the hunger strike

- Prisoners were allowed to wear their own clothes, associate freely, receive more visits and some remission on their sentences was restored.

- The election of Sands and other hunger strikers launched **Sinn Féin** into politics in Northern Ireland. The republican strategy became known as *the armalite in one hand and the ballot box in the other.*

- In 1983, Gerry Adams was elected MP for West Belfast and Sinn Féin candidates gained 13.4% of the vote in Northern Ireland. The SDLP lost votes to Sinn Féin.

- During the same period, IRA violence was stepped up.

- Unionists and nationalists in Northern Ireland grew even further apart.

- Nationalist feeling against Margaret Thatcher's Conservative government increased.

- Concern about increased support for Sinn Féin forced the British and Irish governments to work more closely to find a new solution to the Northern Ireland problem.

(Above) IRA members alongside the coffin of the dead hunger striker, Patsy O'Hara.

(Right) Gerry Adams speaking at a Sinn Féin press conference.

(Below) Anti-IRA poster.

THE I.R.A. ARMY COUNCIL

OR YOUR NEXT DISTRICT COUNCIL?

PUT SINN FEIN OUT OF BUSINESS

VOTE ULSTER UNIONIST ON 15th MAY

KEEP ULSTER BRITISH

1 Why did republican prisoners decide to go on hunger strike in 1980 and 1981?

2 What were the short and longer-term results of the IRA hunger strike?

3 Describe how the following groups might have felt about the hunger strike:

   (a) unionists in Northern Ireland;

   (b) Sinn Féin supporters in Northern Ireland and beyond;

   (c) Catholics in Northern Ireland;

   (d) the British government;

   (e) the hunger strikers.

Anglo-Irish Co-operation

4.13

Focus

What factors brought the British and Irish governments towards closer co-operation in the 1980s?

What effect did the Anglo-Irish Agreement of 1985 have on the way Northern Ireland was governed?

As support for Sinn Féin increased, the British and Irish governments became worried that it might begin to seriously threaten support for the moderate SDLP as the main nationalist party in Northern Ireland.

The New Ireland Forum

The SDLP began looking to Dublin more and more for support for the nationalist community. John Hume, the leader of the SDLP, persuaded the Irish government to hold a conference to discuss the future of Ireland. In the summer of 1983, the New Ireland Forum met in Dublin and was attended by the SDLP and the main nationalist parties in the Republic. Sinn Féin was not invited and the British government and unionists refused to attend the Forum. In May 1984, the New Ireland Forum Report suggested three possible ways forward for Ireland's future. Mrs Thatcher's negative reaction to the Forum report (Source A) reassured unionists.

SOURCE A

British government response to the New Ireland Forum

*A united Ireland was one solution. That is out. A second solution was a confederation of the two states. That is out. A third solution was **joint authority**. That is out.*

Prime Minister Margaret Thatcher, 19 November 1984

(Right) Margaret Thatcher and Garret FitzGerald at the signing the Anglo-Irish Agreement at Hillsborough Castle with Tom King, the Northern Ireland Secretary of State in the background.

Cartoon on the Forum.

The Brighton bomb.

The Anglo-Irish Agreement 1985

In October 1984 the IRA bombed the Conservative Party Conference at Brighton, killing members of the Conservative Party and coming very close to killing the Prime Minister. Soon afterwards, secret meetings took place between the British and Irish governments and a year later the Anglo-Irish Agreement was signed by the British Prime Minister, Margaret Thatcher and Taoiseach, Garret FitzGerald at Hillsborough Castle on 15 November 1985.

In the Agreement:

*   the British government recognised the Republic's right to make proposals on matters relating to Northern Ireland;

*   the Republic recognised a united Ireland was a long-term aim which would only come about with the approval of the majority in Northern Ireland;

*   both governments agreed to try to make Northern Ireland a place where everyone could *live in peace, free from discrimination and intolerance*;

*   both governments agreed to an inter-governmental conference, which would meet regularly to discuss political, legal and security matters;

*   the Agreement was to be reviewed after three years, or earlier, if either government requested it.

On 21 November 1985 the Irish Parliament in Dublin, the Dáil, approved the Anglo-Irish Agreement by 88 votes to 75. Six days later, the House of Commons at Westminster approved the Agreement by 473 to 47 votes. All the main British political parties supported the Agreement. The fact that all the Ulster Unionist MPs were opposed to the Agreement was ignored. After the Anglo-Irish Agreement was signed posters saying 'Mrs Thatcher is a Traitor' appeared in loyalist areas.

SOURCE B

Effigy of Thatcher

SOURCE C

Garret FitzGerald's motives for signing the Anglo-Irish Agreement

*I don't know what the verdict of history will be on the 1985 Agreement. But I can say that in negotiating it I was moved by one purpose: to block the dangerous growth of support for IRA/Sinn Féin during the post hunger strike years 1981–1984, by attempting to create conditions in which northern nationalists could more readily identify with the system of government and security in Northern Ireland. In this way I hoped to weaken support and tolerance of the IRA among part of the northern community, a phenomenon which seemed to me to be a potential major threat to the security of the whole island. Whatever many of you think, the idea of attempting to undermine the right of the people of Northern Ireland to decide the **jurisdiction** under whose sovereignty they wish to live was, and has always been, abhorrent to me.*

Garret FitzGerald, Letter to the unionist community, *The Belfast Newsletter*, 1 September 1994

ACTIVITIES

1 What factors persuaded the Irish government to set up the New Ireland Forum?

2 Why would unionists have been reassured by Source A (page 130), Mrs Thatcher's reaction to the New Ireland Forum Report?

3 Why did many unionists view Mrs Thatcher (Source B) as a traitor after she signed the Anglo-Irish Agreement?

4 What reasons does Garret FitzGerald give in Source C to explain why he signed the Anglo-Irish Agreement? Why might many Protestants find it difficult to accept his explanation?

5 The Anglo-Irish Agreement was passed with one of the largest majorities in the House of Commons this century. Why do you think the Agreement was given so much support?

6 The Fianna Fáil Party in the Republic, led by Charles Haughey, opposed the Anglo-Irish Agreement because it said the Agreement reinforced partition. Choose two points in the Agreement and explain how each might be viewed as reinforcing partition.

Reactions to the Anglo-Irish Agreement

Focus

What was the response to the Anglo-Irish Agreement by the various shades of opinion in Northern Ireland, the Republic and Britain?

The Anglo-Irish Agreement was registered as an international treaty with the United Nations. The international community hoped that the Agreement would help bring a solution to Northern Ireland's problems. The United States, Canada, and New Zealand donated substantial amounts of money to the International Fund for Ireland to help make the Agreement work.

Unionist reaction

The signing of the Anglo-Irish Agreement shocked Northern Ireland's unionists and left them feeling betrayed and abandoned. In their view, Dublin had been given a direct say in the government of their country and a responsibility for looking after the interests of the minority community. Unionists wondered who was now looking after their interests.

Unionist demonstrators outside Hillsborough Castle.

SOURCE A

Unionist response

We are going to be delivered, bound and trussed like a turkey ready for the oven, from one nation to another.

James Molyneaux at a special meeting of the Assembly, 1985

Nationalist reaction

Nationalists in Northern Ireland were divided in their attitude to the Agreement. The SDLP saw it as a chance for progress while Sinn Féin regarded it as reinforcing partition.

SOURCE B

SDLP response

The SDLP welcomes the Anglo-Irish Agreement. It …. presents a major opportunity and challenge to the nationalist people of the north …. It is an opportunity to create equality, justice and fair play for all the people of the north.

West Belfast SDLP pamphlet, December 1985

SOURCE C

Republican response

This deal does not go anywhere near bringing peace to this part of Ireland. On the contrary it reinforces partition because Dublin is recognising Northern Ireland.

Gerry Adams, President of Sinn Féin, 16 November 1985

(Above) Gerry Adams.

(Above right) Mary Robinson.

(Top left) James Molyneaux.

(Top right) Ian Gow.

British and Irish reaction

While the majority of politicians in Britain and the Republic accepted the Agreement, some, like Mary Robinson of the Irish Labour Party (later elected President of the Republic) and Ian Gow, a member of the British government (later killed by the IRA), resigned in protest against it.

SOURCE D

Individual objection within the Conservative Party

The Agreement would never have been signed unless there had been a prolonged campaign of violence .... The involvement of a foreign power in a consultative role in the administration of the province will prolong, and not diminish, Ulster's agony.

Ian Gow, British Treasury Minister, November 1985

SOURCE E

Labour Party response

The Anglo-Irish Agreement, is the reward the gunmen got for their violence. They have created such hatred of insecurity, fear and brutality that they have made nationalists seek change even at the cost of indefinitely postponing a united Ireland.

Neil Kinnock, Leader, 21 November, 1985

SOURCE F

Individual objection within the Irish Labour Party

The Agreement is unacceptable to all sections of unionist opinion. I do not believe it can achieve .... peace and stability within Northern Ireland or on the island as a whole.

Senator Mary Robinson, Irish Labour Party, 18 November 1985

ACTIVITIES

1   What does Source A tell you about unionists' views of the Anglo-Irish Agreement?

2   Using Sources B and C, describe how the SDLP's views of the Anglo-Irish Agreement differed from Sinn Féin's views.

3   Both Sinn Féin and the unionists were opposed to the Anglo-Irish Agreement. In what respects were their reasons for opposing the Agreement different?

4   What did Neil Kinnock (Source E) consider would be the outcome of the Anglo-Irish Agreement? Why might his viewpoint not be shared by unionists?

5   Why did Ian Gow (Source D) and Mary Robinson (Source F) object to the Anglo-Irish Agreement? How do you think northern unionists would have felt about Mary Robinson's resignation? Explain your answer.

Ulster Says No

Focus

Why did the unionist campaign against the Agreement fail?

*The main problem facing unionists was how to get rid of the Anglo-Irish Agreement without further damaging the union with Britain. Most unionists were against using violence. Ian Paisley and James Molyneaux tried to channel unionists' anger into constitutional protest, believing what they called the '**Dublin diktat**' could best be opposed by a campaign of protest and non-co-operation.*

A number of unionist protests against the Agreement took place at the end of 1985, and in early 1986, but the British government paid no attention to them. Unionists became frustrated at being ignored. The increased level of violence and intimidation in 1986 and 1987 was due partly to a loyalist paramilitary campaign against the Agreement. Loyalist paramilitaries saw the RUC as traitors because they knew the government would not be able to make the Agreement work without police support. Attacks on the homes of members of the RUC became common.

(Above) Ian Paisley and James Molyneaux unite to fight Westminster by-elections forced by the resignation of all of Northern Ireland's unionist MPs as a protest against the Anglo-Irish Agreement, 23 January 1986.

(Left) Loyalists picket Harland and Wolff Shipyard on the 'Day of Action', 3 March 1986.

(Below) Ulster Resistance, a paramilitary organisation set up on 10 November 1986 to take direct action (against the Agreement) as and when required.

The campaign fails

By the middle of 1987, unionist opposition to the Anglo-Irish Agreement began to dwindle. Unionists felt they had tried every constitutional method, but were ignored by the British government. Mrs Thatcher's success in the Westminster election, and the review of the Agreement in 1988, left unionists with little hope of change in the foreseeable future. Most people in Northern Ireland realised the campaign to remove the Anglo-Irish Agreement had failed.

(Above) Ian Paisley and James Molyneaux at the Belfast City Hall rally, 23 November 1985.

SOURCE

No Hope Here, *Fortnight* 261, April 1988

1 Describe and attempt to explain the unionist response to what they called the 'Dublin diktat'.

2 Why did Peter Robinson feel unionists needed to be careful in the way they opposed the Agreement (Source A, page 137) and how did the methods unionists employed to oppose the Agreement change between 1985 and 1987?

3 Source B appeared in an independent Belfast magazine in 1988.

   (a) What does the cartoonist show as the reaction to the Anglo-Irish Agreement? Use information from the source to support your answer.

   (b) Does the cartoonist's view of the Anglo-Irish Agreement agree with the views expressed by unionists? Give reasons for your answer.

The Downing Street Declaration

Focus

What action was taken between 1987 and 1993 to try to break the political deadlock in Northern Ireland?

What were the results of these attempts?

In September 1987, James Molyneaux, leader of the Official Unionist Party and Ian Paisley, leader of the Democratic Unionist Party, ended their 19 month boycott of British ministers and agreed to have talks about talks.

Talks about talks

Between 1988 and 1992, numerous attempts were made to get the political parties in Northern Ireland around the table. Differences over the Anglo-Irish Agreement meant the talks made little progress. In March 1991 meetings of the British and Irish Inter-governmental Conference were postponed for ten weeks to allow inter-party discussions to take place on the basis that *nothing was agreed until everything was agreed*. The talks were to operate in three stages:

- Stage One: dealing with the internal government of Northern Ireland;

- Stage Two: dealing with north–south relations;

- Stage Three: dealing with British and Irish relations.

The Stage One talks eventually got underway but little progress was made so the Secretary of State, Peter Brooke, brought the talks to an end. After

(Below left) John Hume (SDLP), Ian Paisley (DUP), Martin Smyth (Ulster Unionist) and John Alderdice (Alliance) arriving at Stormont for talks.

(Below) Peter Brooke.

two years, and a cost of £5 million, the talks process only served to highlight the seemingly irreconcilable differences between nationalism and unionism.

The Hume-Adams initiative

In January 1992, the Deputy President of Sinn Féin, Martin McGuinness, let it be known that Sinn Féin would *make it as easy as possible* for talks to take place between them and the British government. The official British reply was that they could only become involved in talks if Sinn Féin agreed to *a complete cessation of violence.* It was later revealed that the British government and Sinn Féin had secret talks in 1992. In 1993, the SDLP leader, John Hume, held a series of discussions with the Sinn Féin leader, Gerry Adams, as a result of which a document known as the Hume-Adams initiative was presented to both governments. The contents of the document were not revealed and Hume was severely criticised by some sections of the media for talking to those who represented the position of the IRA.

Pointing the way forward: John Major and Albert Reynolds.

The Downing Street Declaration 1993

Three months later the British and Irish governments negotiated and agreed a joint declaration of their mutual position on the future of Northern Ireland which they hoped would create the basis for trust and future agreement between all parties in the conflict. The Downing Street Declaration was announced on 15 December 1993.

BOTH GOVERNMENTS:

- aimed to develop *agreement and reconciliation, leading to a new political framework founded on consent;*

- stated that only political parties with *a commitment to exclusively peaceful methods* would be allowed to join talks;

- accepted that Irish unity could be achieved .... *peacefully and without coercion and violence.*

THE BRITISH GOVERNMENT:

- said it had *no selfish strategic or economic interest in Northern Ireland;*

- promised to work to achieve an agreement *based on full respect for the rights and identities of both traditions in Ireland;*

- accepted the possibility of *a united Ireland achieved by peaceful means;*

- stated *it is for the people of the island of Ireland alone .... to bring about a united Ireland, if that is their wish.*

THE IRISH GOVERNMENT:

- stated *it would be wrong to attempt to impose a united Ireland in the absence of the freely given consent of the majority of the people of Northern Ireland;*

- said *in the event of an overall settlement the Irish government would support proposals for change in the Irish Constitution;*

- agreed to set up a *Forum for Peace and Reconciliation* to find ways to promote agreement and trust between both traditions in Ireland.

SOURCE A

Democratic Unionist Party reaction

You have sold Ulster to buy off the fiendish republican scum.

Ian Paisley, Leader, in a letter to John Major, *The Belfast Telegraph*, 15 December 1993

SOURCE B

Alliance Party reaction

This is a balanced document which gives words of comfort and sensitivity to nationalists and very real structural guarantees to unionists.

John Alderdice, Leader, *The Belfast Telegraph*, 16 December 1993

SOURCE C

Sinn Féin response

Already the general reaction among nationalists is one of disappointment.

Mitchel McLaughlin, Chairman, *The Guardian*, 16 December 1993

ACTIVITIES

1 *Give an account of the events between 1987 and 1993 which may have influenced Anglo-Irish relations.*

2 *Study the main points of the Downing Street Declaration carefully and choose points from it to explain unionist and Sinn Féin reactions to the Declaration as set out in Sources A, B and C.*

Options for the Future

4.17

Focus

What are the main options for an agreed future for Northern Ireland?

After 25 years of violence in which over three thousand people lost their lives, the IRA announced a complete cessation of military operations on Wednesday 31 August 1994. A similar announcement was made by the United Loyalist Command, speaking on behalf of loyalist paramilitary groups, on 13 October 1994. Violence appears to have been set aside for the moment as a means of achieving a change in the way Northern Ireland is governed. All sides agree that there is a need to work towards some form of political settlement.

Background

The following points are generally recognised:

* there are major differences in how the two communities see themselves and how they wish to be governed;

* unionists will not be forced into a united Ireland;

(Above) Time for Peace.

(Left) Belfast shoppers coming to terms with the news of the IRA ceasefire.

- nationalists consider there must be an Irish dimension to the future government of Northern Ireland in order to be guaranteed equal status and the right to pursue the ideal of a United Ireland;

- the British and Irish governments have guaranteed that Northern Ireland will remain within the United Kingdom as long as the majority of people in Northern Ireland wish it to remain so;

- since the Anglo-Irish Agreement in 1985 and the Downing Street Declaration in 1993 the British government have agreed that Dublin will be involved in discussions on the future of Northern Ireland.

The options for a political settlement

Three broad options have been suggested or tried at various times, each with their own difficulties.

1 A purely internal settlement.

2 The joint framework arrangements proposed by the British and Irish Governments.

3 Negotiated structures acceptable to all the political parties.

Option 1: An Internal Settlement

This option would return political power to the elected representatives of Northern Ireland. Because of the difficulties with simple majority rule, a range of different ways of sharing power have been suggested. The major problem with all of the proposed solutions in the past seems to have been a lack of willingness among the main political groupings in Northern Ireland to make power-sharing work. Nationalists, in particular, are unlikely to support a purely internal settlement which does not have an Irish dimension.

Option 2: The Joint Framework Proposals

The Joint Framework Proposals would mean that responsibility for governing Northern Ireland would be shared between a new Northern Ireland Assembly in Belfast and a North/South body, thereby giving Dublin a substantially increased role to influence the way in which Northern Ireland is governed. It is suggested there would be:

1 a 90 member Northern Ireland Assembly in Belfast with responsibility for matters such as, education, health, housing and agriculture. Matters relating to the Crown, foreign affairs and defence would remain at Westminster. A system of committees, set up in proportion to party strengths, would oversee these government departments. An elected panel of three people would oversee and assist the Assembly.

SOURCE A

Reaction to the framework document from the Democratic Unionist Party

This is not a discussion document; this is a declaration of intent – a joint government programme for Irish unity. When the verbal foliage is pruned away, only one central proposition remains and it is entirely a nationalist programme.

Peter Robinson, Deputy Leader, *The Belfast Telegraph*, 22 February 1995

SOURCE B

Reaction to the framework document from the Alliance Party

The document provides a basis for negotiation, not hysteria and alarm. North-South co-operation will be accountable to an Assembly, not the other way round. The Anglo-Irish Conference will be democratised. The Republic will give up its territorial claim and both governments will recognise the principle of consent. Everyone's human rights will be respected.

Dr. John Alderdice, Leader, *The Belfast Telegraph*, 22 February 1995

2   a North-South body made up of elected representatives from the Northern Ireland Assembly and from the Irish Parliament, the Dail which would deal with matters agreed by the two governments and the Northern Ireland political parties, including an agreed approach for the whole island to the European Union.

3   a Parliamentary Forum drawn from the new Assembly and the Dail which would consider matters of mutual interest.

4   a standing British-Irish inter-governmental conference to consider matters of mutual interest.

5   constitutional changes in Irish and UK law to acknowledge the will of a Northern Ireland majority, including the removal of the Republic's territorial claims to Northern Ireland.

6   full protection for specified civil, political, social and cultural rights.

7   a separate referendum, North and South, on the outcomes of any agreement.

The most obvious difficulty with these proposals is the total hostility of unionists to giving any executive power to the Republic of Ireland. An option of this kind might satisfy nationalists, but the declared refusal of unionists to discuss the proposals may make negotiations on this proposed framework extremely difficult.

SOURCE C

Comment on the timing of the Framework document

The memories – and the lessons of the frustrated Sunningdale Agreement and its power-sharing executive, and the Anglo-Irish Agreement, have been learned in Whitehall, despite Unionist claims to the contrary. Why, many wonder, should the government now judge that unionist hostility to an all-Ireland dimension has lessened? Ministers argue that six-months of peace, coupled with Dublin's historic promise of constitutional change are the vital new elements …. Minister believe that the task ahead may, in the words of one, be 'painful, difficult, slow, frustrating'. But they are adamant that the document represents neither a nationalist nor a unionist agenda.

Desmond McCartan, journalist, *The Belfast Telegraph*, 22 February 1995

Option 3: Negotiated Structures Acceptable to All Political Parties

In the wake of the framework document, the most obvious difficulty will be arriving at structures which go far enough to satisfy nationalist expectations and, at the same time, satisfy unionists' concerns about the role given to the Republic of Ireland.

A Republican response to the ceasefire.

SOURCE D

The case for a referendum

The argument for involving the population at large in the process of seeking a compromise is based on the proposition that there is a greater willingness to compromise among large sections of both communities than among their political leaders .... There is some evidence from the hearings of the Opsahl Commission and from recent opinion polls that it may be true. If it is, the two governments should be able to harness sufficient popular support for a package deal to make it difficult either for party leaders to refuse to cooperate with it or for paramilitaries to continue to oppose it. Both the IRA and loyalist paramilitaries claim repeatedly to be acting on behalf of the Irish or the Ulster people and clear evidence in a referendum that a majority in both communities supported a particular settlement would destroy that claim. It would be particularly difficult for the SDLP and Sinn Féin to oppose such a result, provided it was endorsed by an equivalent majority in the Republic of Ireland.

K Boyle and T Hadden, *Northern Ireland: The Choice*, 1994, with the permission of Penguin Books

ACTIVITIES

1 List the pros and cons of each of the three broad options described and give your views on the likelihood of their success.

2 Why does the writer of Source C refer back to the Sunningdale Agreement? What factors do Government Ministers feel may make popular unionist reaction to the Framework document less strong than it was to the Sunningdale Agreement?

3 In what ways do Sources A and B disagree about the intentions behind the framework document and attempt to explain the difference in reaction by reference to the speakers and the parties they represent.

4 To what extent do you feel the suggestions made in Source D is a valid path in the event of political stalemate?

5 In the negotiations about the future of Northern Ireland, outline the range of factors which you feel politicians would need to take into account?

Glossary

Act of Union	An Act passed in 1800 uniting the British and Irish parliaments.
American civil rights movement	A non-violent movement in the early 1960s dedicated to achieving equal treatment for blacks.
amnesty	A general pardon.
Anglo-Irish Treaty, 1921	The treaty which ended the Anglo-Irish War (see below).
Anglo-Irish War/War of Independence	The period 1919-1920 during which the IRA was at war with the British.
annuity payments (land)	Payments to Britain for loans made to tenant farmers in the late 19th century which allowed them to buy the land they worked.
Apprentice Boys	A Protestant organisation which commemorates the apprentice boys of Derry who closed the gates as the siege began.
ascendancy class	Wealthy educated people who were born and lived in Ireland, but considered themselves British.
Auxiliaries	Ex-Army officers who, together with the Black and Tans, joined to reinforce the Royal Irish Constabulary against the IRA in 1920.
B Specials	Part-time members of the Ulster Special Constabulary set up in 1920 to support the regular police force and not disbanded until 1969.
back-to-back streets	Streets in which the backs of houses faced each other, crowding many people into a small area.
Battle of the Somme	Major battle during World War I in which the mainly Protestant 36th Ulster Division suffered extensive casualties.
Black and Tans	Unemployed ex-soldiers recruited to reinforce the Royal Irish Constabulary in their fight against the IRA in 1920.
blackouts	Covering all windows with black curtains and turning off all street lights during World War II creating total darkness to hinder the Germans in their bombing campaign.
blanket protest	A protest by IRA prisoners to gain political status (see below) in which they refused to wear prison clothes and draped themselves with blankets.
Blitz, The	Refers to the German bombing of cities in the United Kingdom, including Belfast and Londonderry in 1941.

Bogside　　　　　　　　A Catholic housing area just outside the walls of Derry.

boycotts　　　　　　　Shunning people to isolate them. Used against RIC men to discourage them from co-operating with the British.

British Conservative Party　　The British mainland party most closely linked to the unionist cause (also called the Conservative and Unionist Party).

Bunreacht na hÉireann　　The name of the 1937 Irish Constitution (in the Irish language).

ceasefire　　　　　　　A cessation of violence by all those engaged in paramilitary activity.

civil war/Civil War　　A war between civilians from the same country. In this context, between those who supported the Anglo-Irish Treaty and those who rejected it.

coalition　　　　　　　An arrangement by which two political parties join together to govern.

Commonwealth　　　　A organisation of former colonies of the United Kingdom with a continuing allegiance to the British Crown.

Communists　　　　　Believers in the theory that society should be classless, that private property should be abolished and that industry should be owned by the state for the benefit of the workers.

compounds　　　　　The name given to the areas in the Maze in which Republican and Loyalist prisoners with political status were held.

Council of Ireland　　After the passing of the Government of Ireland Act 1920, this Council was to be set up with representatives from both north and south to work towards establishing a single parliament for the whole of Ireland.

Cumann na nGaedheal　　Political party formed in the early 1920s after Sinn Féin split as a result of the Anglo-Irish Treaty. (The modern Fine Gael is descended from it.)

curfew　　　　　　　　A time set by which all persons must be indoors. Usually imposed by governments to prevent civil disturbances.

Dáil Éireann　　　　　The lower house in the Irish Parliament The Dáil Éireann would be similar to the House of Commons.

depression/Great Depression　　A period of time during which output of goods and services and employment decline sharply resulting in falling wages, for example, during the 1920s and 1930s.

dirty protest　　　　　A continuation of the blanket protest where IRA prisoners refused to wash or slop out their toilet buckets in protest over the refusal of Britain to grant political status.

discriminate/discrimination	A situation where one group of people is given less access to, for example, education, housing, employment and government because of their beliefs, religion, race or sex.
Dominion status	A self-governing country with connections to the 'mother country' Great Britain and with a Governor General appointed by them.
Dublin diktat	The term unionists gave to the Anglo-Irish Agreement in 1985 which set up inter-governmental conferences and which was signed without their agreement.
Easter Rising, 1916	A rebellion against British rule, in which a small number of Irish Volunteers proclaimed an Irish Republic. The rising was put down and many of its leaders were executed.
economic war	Restrictions on trade between Britain and Ireland between 1932 and 1938 which began in retaliation for de Valera's withholding of annuity payments for land.
External Relations Act, 1936	An act passed by the Irish Parliament which removed the authority of the British Crown in Irish affairs.
'first past the post'	A system of electing candidates using a single non-transferable vote.
flying columns	Small groups of IRA volunteers which launched raids and attacks against Royal Irish Constabulary (RIC) personnel and then escaped by hiding in the community.
franchise	The right to vote.
Free Presbyterian Church	Founded by the Rev Ian Paisley and relying on a literal, fundamentalist interpretation of the Bible.
Free State	The Irish state which was formed after the signing of the Anglo-Irish Treaty.
garrisons	Military establishments containing military personnel on active service.
gerrymandering	The act of fixing unnatural electoral boundaries so that groups of voters are either spread out or bunched together to pre-determine the outcome of any election.
ghetto	An area in which only one group lives, such as Protestants or Catholics, usually associated with poor areas.
Government of Ireland Act, 1920	The act which partitioned Ireland into two states.
H Block	Name given to the prison buildings at the Maze because they were shaped like an 'H'.

hinterland	The part of the country removed from the centre of power or main centre of industry.
Hitler	Leader of the Nazi Party and main Axis power, Germany, in World War II.
Home Rule Party/ movement	A party set up to achieve local government of Ireland within the framework of the United Kingdom.
inter-communal	Between two recognised groups. In this context it refers to problems between the two communities, Protestant and Catholic.
intern/internment	The ability of the government to arrest and hold indefinitely without trial people suspected of acts likely to undermine the government.
Irish Republican Army (IRA)	An organisation that grew out of the Irish Volunteers which took part in the 1916 Easter Uprising and which was ready to use force to create an Irish Republic. Later split into the Official and Provisional IRA.
joint authority	A situation where Northern Ireland would be governed by both the Republic and Britain.
jurisdiction	The area over which any authority extends, for example, Northern Ireland is presently in the jurisdiction of the United Kingdom.
livestock farming	Animal farming, whether cattle, sheep or pigs.
loyalist(s)	Those who totally reject any move away from the union and who have a tendency to accept or use violence to maintain it.
Lundy	Used as a term of abuse to those considered traitors. (Lundy was a Protestant who was a traitor during the Siege of Derry when he attempted to open the gates to the enemy.)
malnutrition	Situation when a person is not eating a proper diet, usually because of not having enough money to purchase healthy food.
Martin Luther King	Black civil rights leader in America who used non-violent, passive resistance and boycotts of white businesses to campaign for equal treatment of blacks.
means tested	A system by which peoples' circumstances were assessed before they were entitled to receive relief.
mortality	Referring to death as a proportion of the population.
multiple voting	The right of ratepayers to have one vote for every ten pounds paid in commercial rates, as well as one vote for rates paid for domestic property.

nationalised (industries)	Those industries which were taken into state ownership and control after World War II by the British government.
nationalist/Nationalist	Those who wished to see Ireland separated from Britain by non-violent means. Also the name of a political party dedicated to achieving these ends.
Ne Temere Decree, 1908	The Decree issued by the Catholic Church in 1908 which denied recognition to marriages between Catholics and Protestants unless they had been solemnised in the Catholic Church and which required children of mixed marriages to be brought up as Catholics.
neutral/neutrality	Neither on one side nor the other, impartial, for example, the position chosen by Eire during World War II.
Oath of Allegiance	An oath that the head of the Irish government had to make to the British Crown (part of the Anglo-Irish Treaty and the 1922 Irish Free State Constitution).
Official IRA	Heirs to the 1920s IRA. After a low-key campaign in 1956–1962 they turned to socialism and political action.
Oireachtas	The name given to the Irish Parliament in the Irish language. This name was agreed in the Irish Free State Constitution of 1922.
Ombudsman	A person appointed by the government to look into complaints. These complaints could be about, for example, housing or employment discrimination.
Orange Order	A Protestant organisation named in honour of William of Orange and dedicated to the continuation of British and Protestant rule in Ireland.
outdoor relief	Hard physical work, such as road mending to achieve a small amount of unemployment benefit, sometimes paid in 'chits' which could only be exchanged for food.
paramilitary/paramilitaries	A group organised along military lines which is prepared to use violence in support of political ideals.
Parliamentary Reform Act, 1918	An Act which increased the categories of those entitled to the vote and which doubled the electorate in Ireland.
partition	The division of one country into two separate countries, in this instance Ireland into the Free State and Northern Ireland.
'points' system	A system for allocating housing fairly, in this context, without reference to an applicant's religion.
political status	An admission by the government that certain prisoners are motivated by political ideals and so are allowed privileges not granted to ordinary criminals.

Poor Law	A system by which each parish supported the poor through the rates.
power-sharing	A system by which all political parties govern together.
Proclamation of the Irish Republic	A proclamation made during the 1916 Easter Rising which declared a republic with no monarchy and no relationship with the United Kingdom.
proportional representation	A system by which voters elect candidates in decreasing order of preference. This system favours smaller parties.
Provisional IRA	Split from the Official IRA in 1970 to form a more militant organisation.
ratepayers	Those who paid rates for homes or business premises. Only ratepayers were entitled to vote in local elections.
rationing	A system of distributing scarce resources fairly, usually involving ration books and coupons.
rent and rates strike	Where tenants and homeowners refuse to pay as a protest against a perceived injustice.
republican(s)	Those who want Northern Ireland to be part of a united Ireland and who have a tendency to accept or use violence to achieve this goal.
republican bonds	Bonds sold by Dáil Éireann to help finance an alternative state after the 1918 election was won by Sinn Féin. (The bond was a promise by the new government to pay back the money lent at a future date plus a small amount of interest.)
rioting	The situation when three or more people disturb the peace by taking to the streets and using violence.
Saorstát na hÉireann	The Free State in the Irish language.
Seanad Éireann	The upper house of the Irish Parliament (Oireachtas), similar to the House of Lords but with both appointed and elected members.
sectarian/sectarianism	When one group injures those of another group for no reason other than that they are perceived as belonging to the other 'side'.
self-determination	The right of small countries to rule themselves, recognised by the Versailles Peace Conference after the end of World War I.
Sinn Féin	The political party set up by Arthur Griffith, meaning Ourselves Alone whose goal was a Republic of Ireland, free from Britain.

soup kitchens	A place for supplying food to the poor. Often set up by charitable organisations or churches.
Taoiseach	The name for the Irish Prime Minister in the Irish language (adopted after the 1937 Irish Constitution came into force).
tariffs	Taxes levied on goods coming into a country to restrict their entry.
tuberculosis (TB)	A lung disease prevalent in the 19th and early to mid 20th centuries associated with poor housing and diet.
Ulster Special Constabulary	See B Specials.
Ulster Volunteer Force (UVF)	A Protestant paramilitary group which takes its name from the organisation set up before World War I, willing to use force to maintain the union.
unionist/Unionist	The position of those upholding the union of Ireland with Britain. Also refers to a political party with the same views usually aligned with the British Conservative Party. After partition refers to the union of Northern Ireland with Britain.
United Irishmen	A group of Irishmen, both Protestant and Catholic, led by Theobald Wolfe Tone and inspired by the French Revolution, which unsuccessfully rebelled against British rule over Ireland in 1798.
Versailles Peace Conference	A conference held after the end of World War I by the victorious allies to determine the borders of countries.
welfare state	The name given to the government plan to set up and pay for a system of care and benefits.
workhouse	A harsh institution set up by the Poor Law where poor people were housed and given food in exchange for work.

Index